W9-BYB-433

Easy to Use

PICK UP & PLAY

HOW TO PLAY

PIANO

& KEYBOARD

SEE IT HEAR IT

ALAN BROWN

EDITED BY JAKE JACKSON

Flame Tree Music

mobile
online
in print

Flame Tree Music
BOOKS • eBOOKS • RESOURCES

Contents

Publisher/Creative Director: Nick Wells • Project, design and media integration: Jake Jackson • Website and software: David Neville with Stevens Dumpala and Steve Moulton • Editorial: Laura Bulbeck

First published 2016 by
FLAME TREE PUBLISHING
6 Melbray Mews, Fulham,
London SW6 3NS, United Kingdom
flametreepublishing.com

Music information site: flametreemusic.com

18 19 20 21 22 • 4 5 6 7 8 9 10

© 2016 Flame Tree Publishing Ltd

The CIP record for this book is available from the British Library.

ISBN: 978-1-78361-958-0

All images and notation courtesy of Flame Tree Publishing Ltd, except the following: keyboard diagrams © 2016 Jake Jackson/Flame Tree Publishing Ltd. Courtesy of Shutterstock.com and copyright the following photographers: Asaf Eliason 155; Monkey Business Images 23; BlackSnake 9; Skylines 15; sagasan 33, 47; BIGCHEN 53; Africa Studio 59, 101; Brad Thompson 60; Murat Subatli 75; JaguarKo & Yevgen Timashov 85; Andi Berger 69; Fotokostic 122; Douglas Freer 125; Vladimir Koletic 160.

In the Public Domain, courtesy of the following: Arjun01 155 & 156 & 157.

Every effort has been made to contact copyright holders. We apologize in advance for any omissions and would be pleased to insert the appropriate acknowledgement in subsequent editions of this publication.

Android is a trademark of Google Inc. Logic Pro, iPhone and iPad are either registered trademarks or trademarks of Apple Computer Inc. in the United States and/or other countries. Cubase is a registered trademark or trademark of Steinberg Media Technologies GmbH, a wholly owned subsidiary of Yamaha Corporation, in the United States and/or other countries. Nokia's product names are either trademarks or registered trademarks of Nokia. Nokia is a registered trademark of Nokia Corporation in the United States and/or other countries. Samsung and Galaxy S are both registered trademarks of Samsung Electronics America, Ltd. in the United States and/or other countries.

This book is an adaptation of Play the Piano Made Easy by Alan Brown, originally published in 2013.

Alan Brown (author) is a former member of the Scottish National Orchestra. He now works as a freelance musician, with several leading UK orchestras, and as a consultant in music and IT. Alan has had several compositions published, developed a set of music theory CD-Roms, co-written a series of bass guitar examination handbooks and worked on over 100 further titles.

Jake Jackson (editor) is a writer and musician. He has created and contributed to over 25 practical music books, including Reading Music Made Easy. His music is available on iTunes, Amazon and Spotify amongst others.

Printed in China

Play the Piano
An Introduction

This book is divided into seven sections. If you follow these, and practise regularly, you should be well on the way to mastering this most versatile of instruments.

1. **All the Basics** introduces notes, finger positions, the staff and clefs (which are used to write music).

2. **Rhythm & Notes** teaches you about the actual written notes. This is your first step into reading real music.

3. **Scales & Accidentals** are important elements of music and this section will show you what these are and how to play and use them.

4. **Intervals & Chords** are also important. They are particularly vital for the left hand as the majority of accompaniments are based in some way on chords.

5. **Arpeggios** are an extension to chords. They are a very useful tool in order to move around the keyboard fluently. You will meet some music that makes particular use of arpeggios and broken chords.

6. **Expression** covers all the elements of a piece of music over and above the pitch and length of the notes. Proper music is so much more than just the notes. This section teaches you the main musical terms in common use so you can understand how a composer wants you to play their music.

7. **Further Techniques** leads you further along the road of performing real music. More key signatures, scales and arpeggios are introduced, as well as a short introduction to flametreemusic.com.

The Diagrams
A Quick Guide

The keyboard diagrams are designed for quick access and ease of use. Whenever you see a keyboard you can use the finger positions and notes to help you make a chord or understand the fingering for a musical example or piece.

Wherever possible the keyboard on the **left** page is for the **left hand**; on the **right** page, the chord is for the **right hand**. This is a great way to learn the structure of the sounds you are making and will help with melodies and solo work. The book repeats these diagrams frequently to help remind you of the notes and positions.

Tabs help give quick access to each section

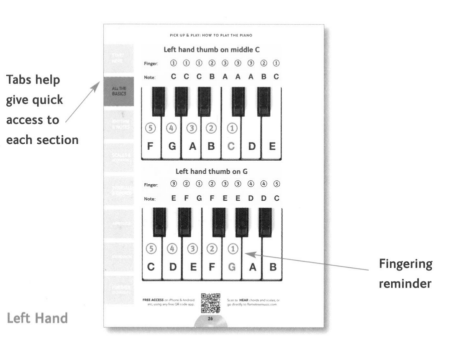

Fingering reminder

Left Hand

FREE ACCESS on iPhone & Android etc, using any free QR code app

Scan to **HEAR** chords and scales, or go directly to flametreemusic.com

Finger positions

Throughout the book the fingers are given numbers:

For the Left Hand :

⑤ ④ ③ ② ①

① is the thumb ② is the index finger
③ is the middle finger ④ is the ring finger
⑤ is the little finger

For the Right Hand:

① ② ③ ④ ⑤

① is the thumb ② is the index finger
③ is the middle finger ④ is the ring finger
⑤ is the little finger

Starting note of the diagram →

Right Hand

Names of the white notes

i. ALL THE BASICS

Right hand thumb on middle C

Finger:	③	②	①	①	③	②	①	①	①
Note:	E	D	C	C	E	D	C	C	C

① ② ③ ④ ⑤
C D E F G A B

Right hand thumb on G

Finger:	①	①	②	②	③	③	③	②	①
Note:	G	G	A	A	B	B	B	A	G

① ② ③ ④ ⑤
F G A B C D E

27

START HERE

ALL THE BASICS

RHYTHM & NOTES

SCALES & ACCIDENTALS

INTERVALS & CHORDS

ARPEGGIOS

EXPRESSION

FURTHER TECHNIQUES

The Sound Links
Another Quick Guide

Requirements: a camera and internet ready smartphone (eg. **iPhone**, any **Android** phone (e.g. **Samsung Galaxy**), **Nokia Lumia**, or **camera-enabled tablet** such as the **iPad Mini**). The best result is achieved using a WIFI connection.

1. Download any **free QR code reader**. An app store search will reveal a great many of these, so obviously it's best to go with the ones with the highest ratings and don't be afraid to try a few before you settle on the one that works best for you. Tapmedia's QR Reader app is good, or ATT Scanner (used below) or QR Media. Some of the free apps have ads, which can be annoying.

2. On your smartphone, open the app and **scan** the **QR code** at the base of any particular page.

FREE ACCESS on iPhone & Android etc, using any free QR code app.

Scan to **HEAR** chords and scales, or go directly to flametreemusic.com

26

3. The QR reader app will take you to a browser, then a specific scale will be displayed on flametreemusic.com.

4. Use the drop down menu to choose from **20 scales** or 12 **free chords** (50 with subscription) per key.

FREE ACCESS on iPhone & Android etc, using any free QR code app

Scan to **HEAR** chords and scales, or go directly to flametreemusic.com

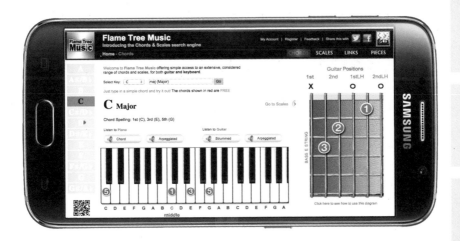

5. Using the usual pinch and zoom techniques, you can focus on four sound options.

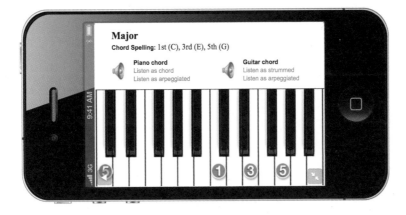

6. Click the sounds! Both piano and guitar audio is provided. This is particularly helpful when you're playing with others.

The QR codes give you direct access to chords and scales. You can access a much wider range of chords if you register and subscribe.

FREE ACCESS on iPhone & Android etc, using any free QR code app

Scan to **HEAR** chords and scales, or go directly to flametreemusic.com

Practising

With any skill, frequency is the key to improvement. Some people will need to spend more time than others, and there are always some for whom it all comes naturally.

How Often Should I Practise?

Ideally you should develop a **daily routine**. Not necessarily all the same things every day, but maybe have a few regular exercises or scales to keep the fingers supple and build up stamina and technique. Then rotate through the pieces you are learning.

How Long Should I Practise For?

As suggested already, frequency is the key to success rather than pure length of practice time. You will progress much faster with **seven daily 20-minute sessions** during the week rather than just one long session of 2 hours and 20 minutes.

You need to balance the length of practice with the time available and the amount of material you are trying to learn. Do not be over-optimistic as you are likely to put it off if you plan sessions that are too long.

For a complete beginner, **10 to 15 minutes every day** is enough. This way it does not become a chore but you are eased in to the idea of practice gently. It should be fun. Build up to half an hour every day.

Don't forget, this is serious **practice** time. Playing through your pieces or improvising should also be done as often as you can make time. This can be just as relaxing as watching TV, and often much more fulfilling.

ALL THE
BASICS

Hands Please

Remember, your audience wants to hear the music – not a clicking of nails on the keys.

You will need to keep your nails reasonably short, but do not over-do it. **Play** the keys with the part of your **finger between** the **tip** and the **pad**.

Your fingers should curve gently on to the keys. Avoid straight fingers, but do not curl them up too much. Imagine your hand is a spider which needs to run along the keyboard. You can go much faster if your **fingers** are **curved** and **relaxed**.

To get the position you are aiming for, try this:

- Let a tennis ball rest in the palm of your hand, with your fingers touching it all round.

- Relax a little and remove the ball.

- Now turn your hand over; this is the position you need.

Scan to **HEAR** chords and scales, or go directly to flametreemusic.com

START HERE

ALL THE BASICS

RHYTHM & NOTES

SCALES & ACCIDENTALS

INTERVALS & CHORDS

ARPEGGIOS

EXPRESSION

FURTHER TECHNIQUES

Notes on the Keyboard

START HERE

ALL THE BASICS

We are now going to have a look at the notes on the keyboard of the instrument.

White Notes

RHYTHM & NOTES

The white notes on the piano are given letter names, but we only use the first seven letters of the standard alphabet.

SCALES & ACCIDENTALS

INTERVALS & CHORDS

ARPEGGIOS

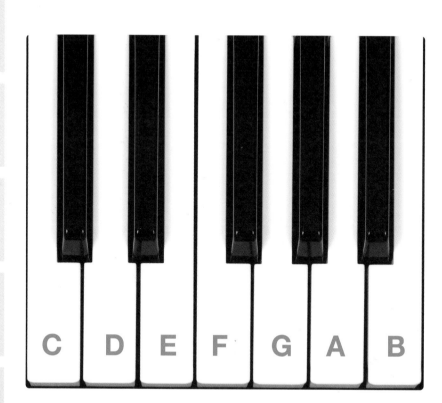

EXPRESSION

FURTHER TECHNIQUES

FREE ACCESS on iPhone & Android
etc, using any free QR code app

Scan to **HEAR** chords and scales, or
go directly to flametreemusic.com

A B C D E F and G

When you get to G you start again from A.

The simplest **major scale** is just **all** the **white notes** played one after the other, but starting from **C**. Try playing these notes and listen to the sound made.

If you play any three alternate notes together then these will make up what we call a **chord**. Try a few and hear what chords sound like.

This one is C major.

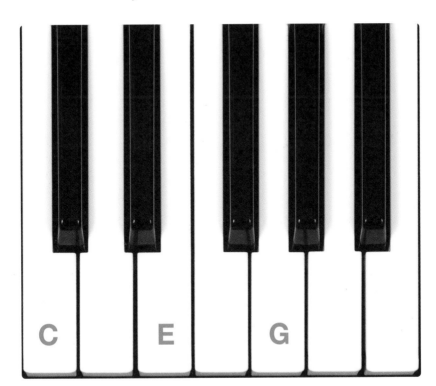

FREE ACCESS on iPhone & Android
etc, using any free QR code app

Scan to **HEAR** chords and scales, or
go directly to flametreemusic.com

Black Notes

In between most of the white notes you will find black notes. These are the sharps and flats.

Sharp sign

Flat sign

START
HERE

ALL THE
BASICS

RHYTHM
& NOTES

SCALES &
ACCIDENTALS

INTERVALS
& CHORDS

ARPEGGIOS

EXPRESSION

FURTHER
TECHNIQUES

START
HERE

ALL THE
BASICS

RHYTHM
& NOTES

SCALES &
ACCIDENTALS

INTERVALS
& CHORDS

ARPEGGIOS

EXPRESSION

FURTHER
TECHNIQUES

All the black notes can be referred to by two different names, depending on the key you are in. This really depends on which main (white) note you want to compare the black note to.

If you want to refer to a note as 'being a little **higher** than F' then you will call it **F sharp**. When you compare it to G (a little **lower** than G) you would call it a **G flat**.

You get '**higher**' by going to the **right** on the keyboard and '**lower**' by going to the **left**.

C♯ D♯   F♯ G♯ A♯

D♭ E♭   G♭ A♭ B♭

C   D   E   F   G   A   B

FREE ACCESS on iPhone & Android etc, using any free QR code app

Scan to **HEAR** chords and scales, or go directly to flametreemusic.com

13

Finger Numbers

We need some way of knowing which finger to use on which note. It would become very difficult to read the music if we used names such as thumb, index finger, and so on. Instead, we give each finger a number. That way, if a note should be played with the middle finger you would see a number 3 above the note on the music.

Both hands have their **thumb** and **fingers** numbered from **1 to 5**, starting with the thumb.

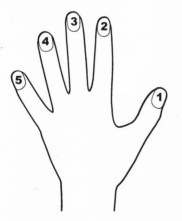
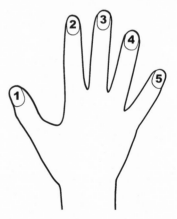

Don't forget, the thumb on both hands is finger number 1 and the little finger is finger number 5.

FREE ACCESS on iPhone & Android etc, using any free QR code app

Scan to **HEAR** chords and scales, or go directly to flametreemusic.com

START HERE

ALL THE BASICS

RHYTHM & NOTES

SCALES & ACCIDENTALS

INTERVALS & CHORDS

ARPEGGIOS

EXPRESSION

FURTHER TECHNIQUES

FREE ACCESS on iPhone & Android etc, using any free QR code app

Scan to **HEAR** chords and scales, or go directly to flametreemusic.com

Finger Numbers for the Left Hand

Left Hand

FREE ACCESS on iPhone & Android etc, using any free QR code app

Scan to **HEAR** chords and scales, or go directly to flametreemusic.com

Finger Numbers for the Right Hand

① ② ③ ④ ⑤

START HERE

ALL THE BASICS

RHYTHM & NOTES

SCALES & ACCIDENTALS

INTERVALS & CHORDS

ARPEGGIOS

EXPRESSION

FURTHER TECHNIQUES

Right Hand

FREE ACCESS on iPhone & Android etc, using any free QR code app

Scan to **HEAR** chords and scales, or go directly to flametreemusic.com

Five-finger Position

Left Hand on the Keyboard

This illustration shows which finger to put on which notes for the **left hand** exercises you will be given shortly.

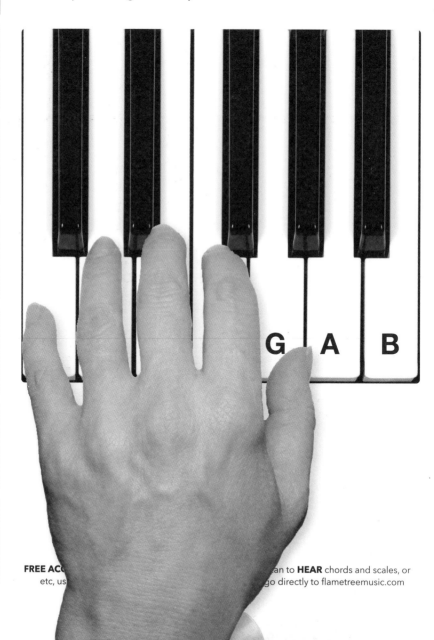

FREE AC... ...an to **HEAR** chords and scales, or etc, us... ...go directly to flametreemusic.com

Navigation tabs:
START HERE
ALL THE BASICS
RHYTHM & NOTES
SCALES & ACCIDENTALS
INTERVALS & CHORDS
ARPEGGIOS
EXPRESSION
FURTHER TECHNIQUES

Right Hand on the Keyboard

This illustration shows which finger to put on which notes for the **right hand** exercises you will be given shortly.

START
HERE

ALL THE
BASICS

RHYTHM
& NOTES

SCALES &
ACCIDENTALS

INTERVALS
& CHORDS

ARPEGGIOS

EXPRESSION

FURTHER
TECHNIQUES

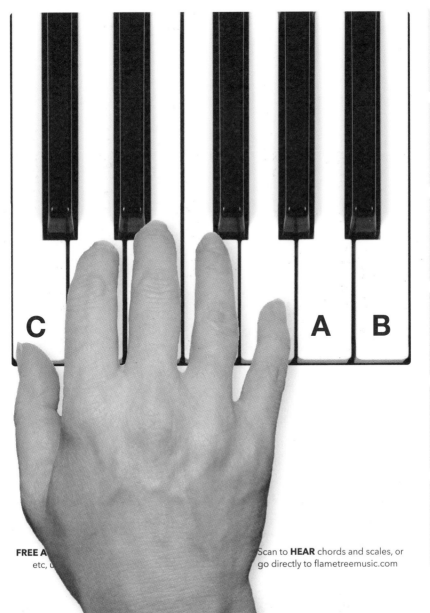

FREE A to HEAR chords and scales, or
etc, u go directly to flametreemusic.com

Very First Tunes

Simple Tunes for the Left Hand

Place your fingers on the keys, then press the finger numbers shown one at a time. The keyboard diagram will help you see which notes should be used.

ALL THE BASICS

Simple Tunes for the Right Hand

Now for the right hand. Place your fingers on the keys, then press the finger numbers shown one at a time.

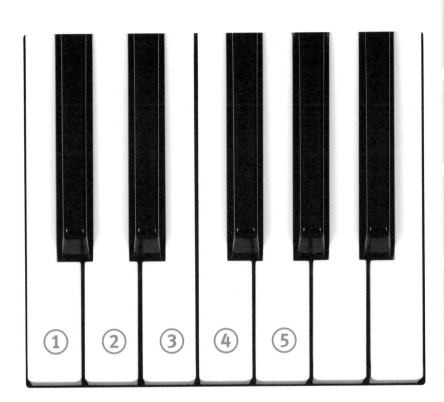

① ② ① ②   ① ② ③ ④   ⑤

③ ② ① ①   ③ ④ ⑤ ⑤   ⑤

⑤ ④ ④ ③   ② ③ ② ②   ①

START HERE

ALL THE BASICS

RHYTHM & NOTES

SCALES & ACCIDENTALS

INTERVALS & CHORDS

ARPEGGIOS

EXPRESSION

FURTHER TECHNIQUES

FREE ACCESS on iPhone & Android etc, using any free QR code app

Scan to **HEAR** chords and scales, or go directly to flametreemusic.com

What We Know So Far

START HERE

ALL THE BASICS

RHYTHM & NOTES

SCALES & ACCIDENTALS

INTERVALS & CHORDS

ARPEGGIOS

EXPRESSION

FURTHER TECHNIQUES

1. You should **always sit comfortably** – not needing to stretch to reach the keys or the pedals.

2. **Fingers** should be **gently curved**.

3. There are white keys with the letter names **A**, **B**, **C**, **D**, **E**, **F** and **G**.

4. Black keys are sometimes called **sharps** and sometimes called **flats**.

5. **Fingers** are **numbered** from 1 to 5, starting with the **thumb** on each hand.

6. **Always warm up** before playing.

7. Practice is more effective when you do **lots of small sessions** rather than one big one.

8. Try to **play every day**.

FREE ACCESS on iPhone & Android etc, using any free QR code app

Scan to **HEAR** chords and scales, or go directly to flametreemusic.com

START
HERE

**ALL THE
BASICS**

RHYTHM
& NOTES

SCALES &
ACCIDENTALS

INTERVALS
& CHORDS

ARPEGGIOS

EXPRESSION

FURTHER
TECHNIQUES

FREE ACCESS on iPhone & Android
etc, using any free QR code app

Scan to **HEAR** chords and scales, or
go directly to flametreemusic.com

Now Try This

Try the simple tunes on the next few pages. We will start off with a few single-hand tunes before we try putting the hands together.

Playing by Numbers

Place your thumb on the note indicated in red, then have one finger per note for the other fingers. When a tune starts on 'middle C', this is the C nearest the middle of your keyboard; if your piano has a lock, then middle C is just near this.

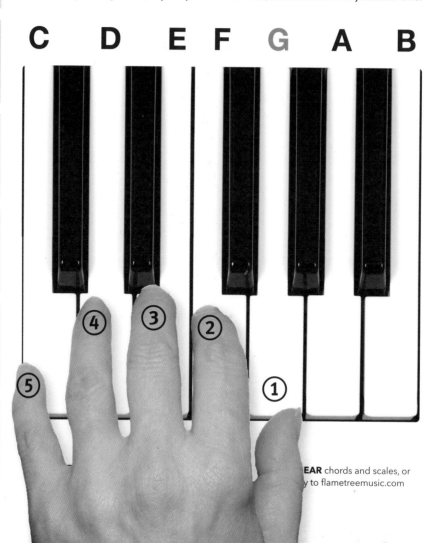

C   D   E   F   G   A   B

EAR chords and scales, or
y to flametreemusic.com

Sidebar navigation:

START HERE

ALL THE BASICS

RHYTHM & NOTES

SCALES & ACCIDENTALS

INTERVALS & CHORDS

ARPEGGIOS

EXPRESSION

FURTHER TECHNIQUES

The first few tunes should be played with even notes – all having the same length. When we come to putting the hands together you will see that the left hand has one note to play while the right hand has four. Hold the left hand finger down while the right hand plays its notes.

The last tunes in this section mix things up, using both hands, with long and short notes. Use these as inspiration for improvising extra bars that complement them, so that it all sounds like one piece. It does not matter where you start on the keyboard for improvisation, the important thing is that you listen to the sound. Try starting on all different notes, maybe even try all black notes.

h to **HEAR** chords and scales, or directly to flametreemusic.com

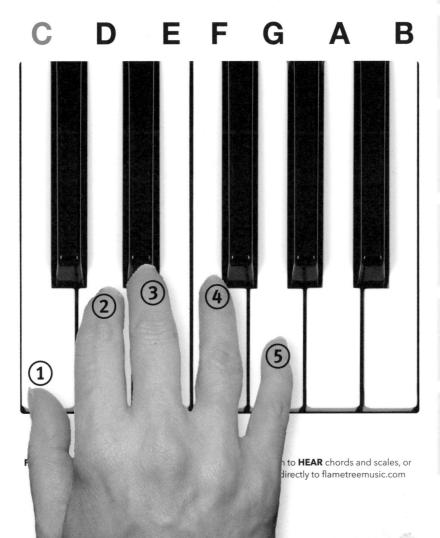

START
HERE

ALL THE
BASICS

RHYTHM
& NOTES

SCALES &
ACCIDENTALS

INTERVALS
& CHORDS

ARPEGGIOS

EXPRESSION

FURTHER
TECHNIQUES

Left hand thumb on middle C

Finger:	①	①	①	②	③	③	③	②	①
Note:	C	C	C	B	A	A	A	B	C

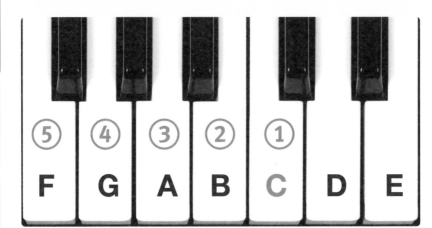

Left hand thumb on G

Finger:	③	②	①	②	③	③	④	④	⑤
Note:	E	F	G	F	E	E	D	D	C

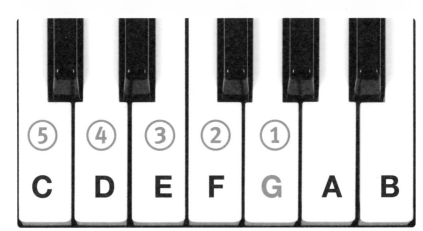

FREE ACCESS on iPhone & Android etc, using any free QR code app

Scan to **HEAR** chords and scales, or go directly to flametreemusic.com

ALL THE BASICS

Right hand thumb on middle C

Finger:	③	②	①	①	③	②	①	①	①
Note:	E	D	C	C	E	D	C	C	C

① C ② D ③ E ④ F ⑤ G A B

Right hand thumb on G

Finger:	①	①	②	②	③	③	③	②	①
Note:	G	G	A	A	B	B	B	A	G

F ① G ② A ③ B ④ C ⑤ D E

START HERE

ALL THE BASICS

RHYTHM & NOTES

SCALES & ACCIDENTALS

INTERVALS & CHORDS

ARPEGGIOS

EXPRESSION

FURTHER TECHNIQUES

FREE ACCESS on iPhone & Android etc, using any free QR code app

Scan to **HEAR** chords and scales, or go directly to flametreemusic.com

START
HERE

ALL THE
BASICS

RHYTHM
& NOTES

SCALES &
ACCIDENTALS

INTERVALS
& CHORDS

ARPEGGIOS

EXPRESSION

FURTHER
TECHNIQUES

Now with hands together, but using the same finger on each hand at the same time.

Both thumbs on middle C

R finger:	①	①	①	②	③	③	③	②	①
R note:	C	C	C	D	E	E	E	D	C
L finger:	①	①	①	②	③	③	③	②	①
L note:	C	C	C	B	A	A	A	B	C

Right hand thumb on a high G, left hand thumb on a low G

R finger:	①	③	⑤	③	④	③	②	②	①
R note:	G	B	D	B	C	B	A	A	G
L finger:	①	③	⑤	③	④	③	②	②	①
L note:	G	E	C	E	D	E	F	F	G

FREE ACCESS on iPhone & Android
etc, using any free QR code app

Scan to **HEAR** chords and scales, or
go directly to flametreemusic.com

Hands together again, playing the same note with each hand at the same time.

Right hand thumb on middle C,
left hand thumb on G

R finger:	①	①	②	②	③	③	④	⑤	①
R note:	**C**	**C**	**D**	**D**	**E**	**E**	**F**	**G**	**C**
L finger:	⑤	⑤	④	④	③	③	②	①	⑤
L note:	**C**	**C**	**D**	**D**	**E**	**E**	**F**	**G**	**C**

Right hand thumb on G,
left hand thumb on D

R finger:	①	⑤	①	⑤	①	③	⑤	③	①
R note:	**G**	**D**	**G**	**D**	**G**	**B**	**D**	**B**	**G**
L finger:	⑤	①	⑤	①	⑤	③	①	③	⑤
L note:	**G**	**D**	**G**	**D**	**G**	**B**	**D**	**B**	**G**

START HERE

ALL THE BASICS

RHYTHM & NOTES

SCALES & ACCIDENTALS

INTERVALS & CHORDS

ARPEGGIOS

EXPRESSION

FURTHER TECHNIQUES

FREE ACCESS on iPhone & Android etc, using any free QR code app

Scan to **HEAR** chords and scales, or go directly to flametreemusic.com

Hands together, but now the left hand is playing long notes.

Right hand thumb on middle C, left hand thumb on G

R finger:	③	②	③	②	⑤	④	⑤	④	①
R note:	E	D	E	D	G	F	G	F	C
L finger:	⑤				①				⑤
L note:	C				G				C

Right hand thumb on middle D, left hand thumb on A

R finger:	①	①	②	③	⑤	⑤	④	②	①
R note:	D	D	E	F	A	A	G	E	D
L finger:	⑤			①		①			⑤
L note:	D			A		A			D

FREE ACCESS on iPhone & Android etc, using any free QR code app

Scan to **HEAR** chords and scales, or go directly to flametreemusic.com

Now let's mix all these things up.

Right hand thumb on middle C, left hand thumb on G

R finger:	③	④	③	②	③	⑤	③	②	①
R note:	E	F	E	D	E	G	E	D	C
L finger:	③	④	③	②	①		①		⑤
L note:	E	D	E	F	G		G		C

Right hand thumb on a very high A, left hand thumb on a very low E

R finger:	①	①	⑤	⑤	③	③	⑤	⑤	①
R note:	A	A	E	E	C	C	E	E	A
L finger:	⑤	⑤	①	①	③	③	①		⑤
L note:	A	A	E	E	C	C	E		A

START HERE

ALL THE BASICS

RHYTHM & NOTES

SCALES & ACCIDENTALS

INTERVALS & CHORDS

ARPEGGIOS

EXPRESSION

FURTHER TECHNIQUES

FREE ACCESS on iPhone & Android etc, using any free QR code app

Scan to **HEAR** chords and scales, or go directly to flametreemusic.com

The Staff

Music is written on a series of five lines, called the stave or staff. The notes are either placed on a line or in a space to indicate which pitch to play.

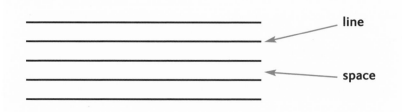

For piano, we use two sets of these lines: **one** for the **right** hand and **one** for the **left** hand. They are placed one above the other and are bracketed together to show that the hands play together.

START HERE

ALL THE BASICS

RHYTHM & NOTES

SCALES & ACCIDENTALS

INTERVALS & CHORDS

ARPEGGIOS

EXPRESSION

FURTHER TECHNIQUES

FREE ACCESS on iPhone & Android etc, using any free QR code app

Scan to **HEAR** chords and scales, or go directly to flametreemusic.com

Music is read the same way as words on a page – from left to right, then down the page starting at the top.

The music is grouped into **bars**, and you will see vertical lines regularly throughout the music. This makes the music easier to follow and also indicates the basic rhythmic pulse, but we will go in to that later.

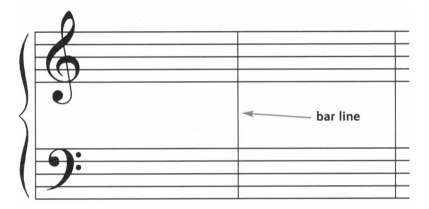

bar line

Scan to **HEAR** chords and scales, or go directly to flametreemusic.com

START HERE

ALL THE BASICS

RHYTHM & NOTES

SCALES & ACCIDENTALS

INTERVALS & CHORDS

ARPEGGIOS

EXPRESSION

FURTHER TECHNIQUES

The Treble Clef

START
HERE

ALL THE
BASICS

RHYTHM
& NOTES

SCALES &
ACCIDENTALS

INTERVALS
& CHORDS

ARPEGGIOS

EXPRESSION

FURTHER
TECHNIQUES

There are special symbols to indicate the type of staff being used: five static lines are not enough to cover the whole piano. We will only need to learn two symbols for the piano.

The first symbol is the **treble clef**. It is generally used for the right hand. It is used for **music above middle C**.

FREE ACCESS on iPhone & Android etc, using any free QR code app

Scan to **HEAR** chords and scales, or go directly to flametreemusic.com

START HERE

ALL THE BASICS

RHYTHM & NOTES

SCALES & ACCIDENTALS

INTERVALS & CHORDS

ARPEGGIOS

EXPRESSION

FURTHER TECHNIQUES

Middle C is the C on the keyboard closest to the **middle** of the **keyboard**.

Middle C

The treble clef is sometimes called the '**G clef**' because you start to draw it from the **G line** on the stave. You will learn the names of the lines and spaces shortly.

FREE ACCESS on iPhone & Android etc, using any free QR code app

Scan to **HEAR** chords and scales, or go directly to flametreemusic.com

The Lines of the Treble Clef

The names of the five lines in the treble clef are (starting from the lowest) E, G, B, D and F. See if you can find these notes on your keyboard.

It is difficult to remember the letters to begin with so we often use a simple phrase to remind us, with the first letter of each word being the letter name of the line.

START
HERE

ALL THE
BASICS

RHYTHM
& NOTES

SCALES &
ACCIDENTALS

INTERVALS
& CHORDS

ARPEGGIOS

EXPRESSION

FURTHER
TECHNIQUES

Here are two common phrases. Pick your favourite, or make up your own by filling in the gaps below.

Every Green Bus Drives Fast

Every Good Boy Deserves Football

E _ _ _ G _ _ _ B _ _ _ D _ _ _ F _ _ _

Here is a note on a line:

The Spaces of the Treble Clef

As with the lines, we need a way of remembering the spaces between the lines.

There are just **four spaces** and in the **treble clef** they just happen to make up a word:

F   A   C   E

This is an easy one to remember.

START HERE

ALL THE BASICS

RHYTHM & NOTES

SCALES & ACCIDENTALS

INTERVALS & CHORDS

ARPEGGIOS

EXPRESSION

FURTHER TECHNIQUES

FREE ACCESS on iPhone & Android etc, using any free QR code app

Scan to **HEAR** chords and scales, or go directly to flametreemusic.com

Try playing all these four notes together on the piano – they make quite a nice sound. A **chord**.

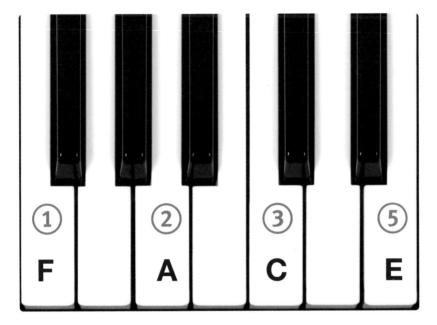

Here is what a note in a **space** looks like:

The Bass Clef

For the lower notes we need to use a different clef. The bass clef covers the notes below middle C and is generally used for the left hand.

On the piano we need to know both the treble and bass clefs as we can play both high and low notes, using the left and right hands.

Many other instruments just use one of the clefs as they can only play high or only play low. Look at these instruments below, then see if you can work out whether they will use the treble or bass clef.

The bass clef is sometimes known as the F clef as you begin to draw it from **the F line** on the stave.

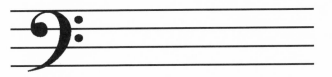

START HERE

ALL THE BASICS

RHYTHM & NOTES

SCALES & ACCIDENTALS

INTERVALS & CHORDS

ARPEGGIOS

EXPRESSION

FURTHER TECHNIQUES

The Lines of the Bass Clef

As with the treble clef, we need a way to remember the names of the **five lines** of the bass clef.

They are **different** to the treble clef – the bass clef lines (starting at the bottom) are:

G B D F A

This one is not so easy to remember, but just as important.

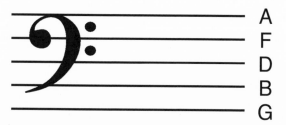

Here are some phrases to help you remember them:

Good Boys Don't Forget Anything

Good Boys Do Fine Always

Why not try to make up your own?

G _ _ _ B _ _ _ D _ _ _ F _ _ _ A _ _ _

Here is a note on a **line**:

ALL THE
BASICS

The Spaces of the Bass Clef

START
HERE

ALL THE
BASICS

We also need a way of remembering the spaces.

As in the treble clef, there are just **four spaces** in the **bass clef**, starting at the bottom.

RHYTHM
& NOTES

A C E G

SCALES &
ACCIDENTALS

This is also an easy one to remember.

INTERVALS
& CHORDS

ARPEGGIOS

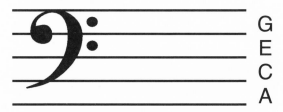

EXPRESSION

FURTHER
TECHNIQUES

FREE ACCESS on iPhone & Android
etc, using any free QR code app

Scan to **HEAR** chords and scales, or
go directly to flametreemusic.com

Here are some phrases to help you remember them:

All Cows Eat Grass

All Cars Eat Gas

Now try to make up your own.

A _ _ _   C _ _ _   E _ _ _   G _ _ _

Here is a note in a space:

START
HERE

ALL THE
BASICS

RHYTHM
& NOTES

SCALES &
ACCIDENTALS

INTERVALS
& CHORDS

ARPEGGIOS

EXPRESSION

FURTHER
TECHNIQUES

FREE ACCESS on iPhone & Android
etc, using any free QR code app

Scan to **HEAR** chords and scales, or
go directly to flametreemusic.com

Skips and Steps

Music is made up of notes moving step by step at different speeds or by jumping over notes, often called skipping.

It is important to get to know both these things, and the following pages have some exercises for you to try.

For the **step-by-step** exercises, place the finger indicated on the starting note then try to use just one finger per note **without moving your hand** at all during the exercise.

For the **skipping exercises**, try two methods.

1. Firstly try to play all the notes by hardly moving the hand – stretch for the notes.

2. Then try skipping along the notes using just one to two fingers.

How about trying each one five times, once for each finger?

FREE ACCESS on iPhone & Android etc, using any free QR code app

Scan to **HEAR** chords and scales, or go directly to flametreemusic.com

START HERE

ALL THE BASICS

RHYTHM & NOTES

SCALES & ACCIDENTALS

INTERVALS & CHORDS

ARPEGGIOS

EXPRESSION

FURTHER TECHNIQUES

FREE ACCESS on iPhone & Android etc, using any free QR code app

Scan to **HEAR** chords and scales, or go directly to flametreemusic.com

START
HERE

ALL THE
BASICS

RHYTHM
& NOTES

SCALES &
ACCIDENTALS

INTERVALS
& CHORDS

ARPEGGIOS

EXPRESSION

FURTHER
TECHNIQUES

Right Hand Steps

Place your thumb on G

Place your thumb on A

Right Hand Skips

Place your thumb on E

Place your thumb on B

FREE ACCESS on iPhone & Android
etc, using any free QR code app

Scan to **HEAR** chords and scales, or
go directly to flametreemusic.com

Left Hand Steps

Place your thumb on G

Place your thumb on D

Left Hand Skips

Place your thumb on F

Place your thumb on G

Scan to **HEAR** chords and scales, or go directly to flametreemusic.com

START
HERE

**ALL THE
BASICS**

RHYTHM
& NOTES

SCALES &
ACCIDENTALS

INTERVALS
& CHORDS

ARPEGGIOS

EXPRESSION

FURTHER
TECHNIQUES

Steps and Skips for Right Hand

Start with your thumb on G, but watch out for the big jumps at the end.

FREE ACCESS on iPhone & Android
etc, using any free QR code app

Scan to **HEAR** chords and scales, or
go directly to flametreemusic.com

START
HERE

ALL THE
BASICS

RHYTHM
& NOTES

SCALES &
ACCIDENTALS

INTERVALS
& CHORDS

ARPEGGIOS

EXPRESSION

FURTHER
TECHNIQUES

Steps and Skips for Left Hand

Start with your thumb on G, but watch out for the big jumps at the end.

START
HERE

ALL THE
BASICS

RHYTHM
& NOTES

SCALES &
ACCIDENTALS

INTERVALS
& CHORDS

ARPEGGIOS

EXPRESSION

FURTHER
TECHNIQUES

FREE ACCESS on iPhone & Android
etc, using any free QR code app

Scan to **HEAR** chords and scales, or
go directly to flametreemusic.com

Playing by Ear

START
HERE

ALL THE
BASICS

RHYTHM
& NOTES

SCALES &
ACCIDENTALS

INTERVALS
& CHORDS

ARPEGGIOS

EXPRESSION

FURTHER
TECHNIQUES

There are times when written music is not available. For example, you might hear a piece of music at a concert and want to play it yourself. Or maybe a friend has worked out a great song but doesn't know how to write music. This is where playing by ear is a useful skill.

As the term implies, your ear is as important as your fingers. You need to listen carefully to the music played, then try to copy it on the piano.

Here are some specific things to ask yourself:

1. **Is the music high or low?**

2. **Is the music fast or slow?**

3. **Do the notes move step by step or skip along?**

4. **How far apart do the notes sound?**

FREE ACCESS on iPhone & Android
etc, using any free QR code app

Scan to **HEAR** chords and scales, or
go directly to flametreemusic.com

START
HERE

**ALL THE
BASICS**

Create a **shape** in your mind then try to recreate this on the piano.

The exercises on the following pages give you some practice at playing by ear; the first stage of creating a **shape diagram** has been done for you.

Try starting on a **different note each time** you play these shapes.

You might come across these tunes later in this book, so be on the lookout!

RHYTHM
& NOTES

SCALES &
ACCIDENTALS

INTERVALS
& CHORDS

ARPEGGIOS

EXPRESSION

FURTHER
TECHNIQUES

FREE ACCESS on iPhone & Android
etc, using any free QR code app

Scan to **HEAR** chords and scales, or
go directly to flametreemusic.com

Left Hand Tunes

Gently flowing

Jumping around

Steps in groups

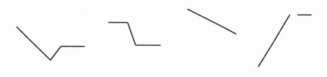

Where you see a horizontal, play the same note several times.

ALL THE
BASICS

START
HERE

RHYTHM
& NOTES

SCALES &
ACCIDENTALS

INTERVALS
& CHORDS

ARPEGGIOS

EXPRESSION

FURTHER
TECHNIQUES

Right Hand Tunes

Gently flowing

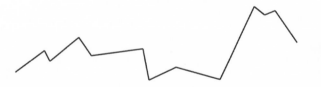

Jumping around

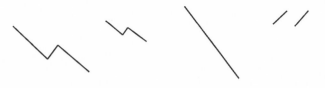

Steps in groups

Where there is a gap, jump to a new starting note.

START
HERE

**ALL THE
BASICS**

RHYTHM
& NOTES

SCALES &
ACCIDENTALS

INTERVALS
& CHORDS

ARPEGGIOS

EXPRESSION

FURTHER
TECHNIQUES

Tunes for Both Hands

Echoes

Copy what the right hand played in the left hand.

Jumping together

Move exactly the same with each hand.

Black note bounce

Repeat each note a few times (longer lines mean more repeats).
Share this tune between your hands.

START HERE

ALL THE BASICS

RHYTHM & NOTES

SCALES & ACCIDENTALS

INTERVALS & CHORDS

ARPEGGIOS

EXPRESSION

FURTHER TECHNIQUES

Question and Answer

Here are the beginnings of four phrases. Make up a **second half** for each so that it either copies or mirrors the start you are given.

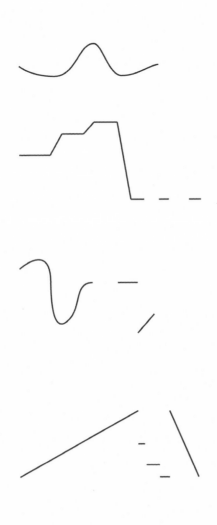

What We Know So Far

We have gone a long way from just playing by numbers. You can now read music and play by ear. Here is a reminder of what you should know:

ALL THE BASICS

1. Music is written on five lines called a stave or a **staff**.

2. Notes are either on the **lines** or in the **spaces**.

3. Every line and every space has a **letter name**.

4. The higher notes are written on a staff with a **treble** clef.

5. The lower notes are written on a staff with a **bass** clef.

6. You have learned **phrases** to remind you of the letter names of the lines and spaces.

7. Playing by ear involves **listening** carefully to the music and creating a melodic 'shape'.

8. Music moves from note to note either **step by step** or by **skipping** from one note to the next.

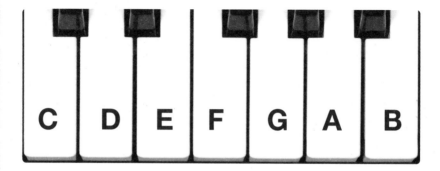

FREE ACCESS on iPhone & Android etc, using any free QR code app

Scan to **HEAR** chords and scales, or go directly to flametreemusic.com

ALL THE
BASICS

FREE ACCESS on iPhone & Android
etc, using any free QR code app

Scan to **HEAR** chords and scales, or
go directly to flametreemusic.com

Now Try This

START HERE

ALL THE BASICS

RHYTHM & NOTES

SCALES & ACCIDENTALS

INTERVALS & CHORDS

ARPEGGIOS

EXPRESSION

FURTHER TECHNIQUES

The next few pages introduce some simple tunes using everything you have learned so far.

To make the tunes more interesting we need to know how long to hold a note down for. We will be learning about all the different notes, their names and their lengths soon.

Do not worry too much about timing and rhythm at the moment – this section is all about **practising** the **notes**.

FREE ACCESS on iPhone & Android etc, using any free QR code app

Scan to **HEAR** chords and scales, or go directly to flametreemusic.com

START
HERE

ALL THE
BASICS

RHYTHM
& NOTES

SCALES &
ACCIDENTALS

INTERVALS
& CHORDS

ARPEGGIOS

EXPRESSION

FURTHER
TECHNIQUES

We will use two types of note, a short note and a long note:

Short Note

crotchet

Long Note

minim

Try all these tunes at different speeds to find the version you like most.

Right Hand Tune

Mouse Dance

Starts with middle finger on E

FREE ACCESS on iPhone & Android etc, using any free QR code app

Scan to **HEAR** chords and scales, or go directly to flametreemusic.com

Left Hand Tune

Elephant Dance

Starts with little finger on G

Scan to **HEAR** chords and scales, or
go directly to flametreemusic.com

START HERE

ALL THE
BASICS

RHYTHM
& NOTES

SCALES &
ACCIDENTALS

INTERVALS
& CHORDS

ARPEGGIOS

EXPRESSION

FURTHER
TECHNIQUES

Keeping a Steady Pulse

Most music has a steady pulse. You need to keep this pulse going whilst you play the music.

All notes have lengths which are related to the pulse.

Think of a clock ticking – this is a steady pulse.

A metronome will provide you with a steady pulse, and you can set this to a wide variety of speeds.

Try setting your metronome going then clapping along with it.

Make sure your clap is at exactly the same time as the metronome's click, not just after it.

A good sense of rhythm is important.

It makes your playing much more musical and enjoyable to listen to. And it is essential if you want to play along with others.

START HERE

ALL THE BASICS

RHYTHM & NOTES

SCALES & ACCIDENTALS

INTERVALS & CHORDS

ARPEGGIOS

EXPRESSION

FURTHER TECHNIQUES

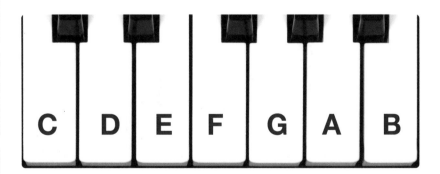

FREE ACCESS on iPhone & Android etc, using any free QR code app

Scan to **HEAR** chords and scales, or go directly to flametreemusic.com

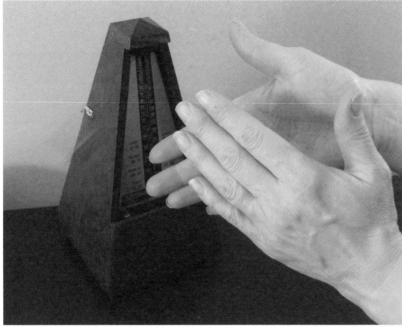

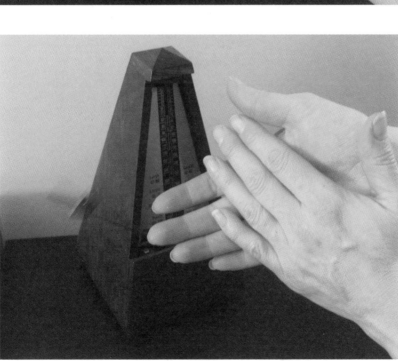

START
HERE

ALL THE
BASICS

RHYTHM
& NOTES

SCALES &
ACCIDENTALS

INTERVALS
& CHORDS

ARPEGGIOS

EXPRESSION

FURTHER
TECHNIQUES

FREE ACCESS on iPhone & Android
etc, using any free QR code app

Scan to **HEAR** chords and scales, or
go directly to flametreemusic.com

Try these exercises:

1. With your **left hand**, tap a steady pulse on the table top. Use a metronome to help if necessary.

2. Now, whilst your left hand continues as the same speed, **tap** with your **right hand** in the following ways:

   - Both hands tapping at exactly the same time

   - Right hand taps exactly twice as fast as the left

   - Right hand taps between the left hand taps

3. Now try **reversing** the hands over, so the right hand has the main beat.

Here are a few more complicated rhythms:

For each of them, the left hand should keep a steady pulse whilst the right hand fits in. Again, try swapping the hands over when you have got the hang of it.

The red dots should be the loudest.

Accented beat. ✪

Standard beat. ✪

RH: ⭐ ⭐ ⭐ ⭐ ⭐

LH: ⭐ ⭐ ⭐ ⭐

RH: ⭐ ⭐ ⭐ ⭐ ⭐

LH: ⭐ ⭐ ⭐ ⭐

RH: ⭐ ⭐ ⭐ ⭐ ⭐

LH: ⭐ ⭐ ⭐ ⭐

RH: ⭐ ⭐ ⭐ ⭐ ⭐

LH: ⭐ ⭐ ⭐ ⭐

RH: ⭐ ⭐ ⭐ ⭐ ⭐ ⭐ ⭐ ⭐ ⭐

LH: ⭐ ⭐ ⭐ ⭐

RH: ⭐ ⭐ ⭐ ⭐ ⭐ ⭐ ⭐ ⭐ ⭐

LH: ⭐ ⭐ ⭐ ⭐

START HERE

ALL THE BASICS

RHYTHM & NOTES

SCALES & ACCIDENTALS

INTERVALS & CHORDS

ARPEGGIOS

EXPRESSION

FURTHER TECHNIQUES

FREE ACCESS on iPhone & Android etc, using any free QR code app

Scan to **HEAR** chords and scales, or go directly to flametreemusic.com

Note Values

All notes have a length or value – often referred to as how many counts they last for.

Most of the time we use the **quarter note** (**crotchet**) as the basis for counting – this note is introduced shortly.

A **quarter note (crotchet)** lasts for **one count** and other notes are said to be 2 counts, 4 counts, half a count, etc.

To begin with we will just learn the four most important note values – these will be sufficient to play a lot of different tunes.

An important thing to remember is that all bars should be filled up – if your music has a **pulse** 'in 4' then you will need note values totaling 4 in every bar.

A single 4-count note or two 2-count notes for example.

FREE ACCESS on iPhone & Android etc, using any free QR code app

Scan to **HEAR** chords and scales, or go directly to flametreemusic.com

START
HERE

ALL THE
BASICS

RHYTHM
& NOTES

SCALES &
ACCIDENTALS

INTERVALS
& CHORDS

ARPEGGIOS

EXPRESSION

FURTHER
TECHNIQUES

There are two naming systems for the notes; choose which one you prefer.

American, **jazz** and **popular** terminology tends to prefer names like **whole note**, **quarter note**, etc.

Classical music uses words such as **semibreve**, **crotchet**, etc.

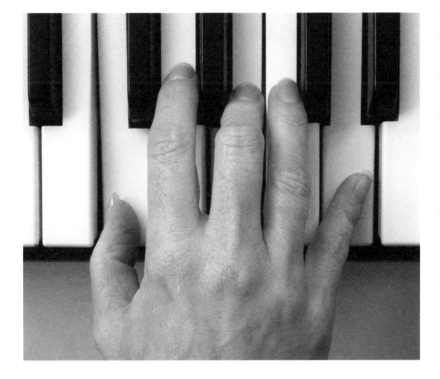

FREE ACCESS on iPhone & Android etc, using any free QR code app

Scan to **HEAR** chords and scales, or go directly to flametreemusic.com

Whole Note/Semibreve

A **whole note (semibreve)** lasts for **4 counts**. It **fills** a standard **bar**, hence the name 'whole note'.

Here are a few bars of whole notes (semibreves).

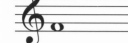

Half Note/Minim

A **half note (minim)** lasts for **2 counts**. You need two of these to fill a standard bar. **A half note** (**minim**) is **half** the length of a **whole note (semibreve)**.

Here are a few bars of half notes (minims).

START HERE

ALL THE BASICS

RHYTHM & NOTES

SCALES & ACCIDENTALS

INTERVALS & CHORDS

ARPEGGIOS

EXPRESSION

FURTHER TECHNIQUES

Quarter Note/Crotchet

A **quarter note (crotchet)** lasts for **1 count**. You need **four** of these to **fill** a standard **bar**. A quarter note (crotchet) is **half** the length of a **half note (minim)**.

Here are a few bars of quarter notes (crotchets).

Scan to **HEAR** chords and scales, or go directly to flametreemusic.com

Eighth Note/Quaver

A **single eighth note (quaver)** looks slightly different when written on its own and when there are several written together. When written together, their tails join together to make a beam.

START
HERE

ALL THE
BASICS

RHYTHM
& NOTES

SCALES &
ACCIDENTALS

INTERVALS
& CHORDS

ARPEGGIOS

EXPRESSION

FURTHER
TECHNIQUES

An **eighth note (quaver)** lasts for **half** a count. You need **eight** of these to **fill** a standard **bar**. An eighth note (quaver) is **half** the length of a **quarter note (crotchet)**.

Quavers are often grouped together in twos or fours. Here are a few bars of eighth notes (quavers).

Rests

As was mentioned in the section about notes, a bar needs to be filled – you cannot leave a gap.

So what do we do when we want a silence in the music?

This is where rests come in – they are actually place holders for silent beats. This way, you will know exactly how long to wait before playing the next note.

For **every note** there is an **equivalent rest**.

We have just learned four common notes, now let's meet **the four rests**.

We will see some examples of:

whole note rest
half note rest
quarter note rest
eighth note rest.

The **alternative** terms for these are

semibreve rest
minim rest
crotchet rest
quaver rest.

START
HERE

ALL THE
BASICS

RHYTHM
& NOTES

SCALES &
ACCIDENTALS

INTERVALS
& CHORDS

ARPEGGIOS

EXPRESSION

FURTHER
TECHNIQUES

FREE ACCESS on iPhone & Android
etc, using any free QR code app

Scan to **HEAR** chords and scales, or
go directly to flametreemusic.com

Whole Note Rest/Semibreve Rest

A whole note rest (semibreve rest) lasts for **4 counts**.

The whole note rest is also used to indicate **a whole bar rest** – so if we have bars which are only 3 beats long, this rest will actually last for three beats in this case.

Half Note Rest/Minim Rest

A half note rest (minim rest) lasts for **2 counts**.

You need **two** of these to **fill** a **standard bar**.

A half note rest (minim rest) is half the length of a whole note rest (semibreve rest).

Quarter Note Rest/Crotchet Rest

A quarter note rest (crotchet rest) lasts for **1 count**.

You need four of these to fill a standard bar.

A quarter note rest (crotchet rest) is half the length of a half note rest (minim rest).

Eighth Note Rest/Quaver Rest

An eighth note rest (quaver rest) lasts for **half a count**.

An eighth note rest (quaver rest) is half the length of a quarter note rest (crotchet rest).

You will not normally see a lot of these together – if you need two eighth note rests (quaver rests) together then you would often write a quarter note rest (crotchet rest).

START HERE

ALL THE BASICS

RHYTHM & NOTES

SCALES & ACCIDENTALS

INTERVALS & CHORDS

ARPEGGIOS

EXPRESSION

FURTHER TECHNIQUES

Here are some tunes using rests. Remember to hold the notes down for their full length.

Rest A While

Bouncing Tops

Remember also to make sure there is silence for the length of the rests.

Copy Cat

Waiting Tune

START
HERE

ALL THE
BASICS

RHYTHM
& NOTES

SCALES &
ACCIDENTALS

INTERVALS
& CHORDS

ARPEGGIOS

EXPRESSION

FURTHER
TECHNIQUES

Ties

START
HERE

ALL THE
BASICS

Sometimes we need a note to last longer than a standard note length or maybe even longer than a whole bar. We can increase the length of a note by tying two notes together. The symbol used is a curved line which joins the note heads and it is called a 'tie'.

RHYTHM
& NOTES

To make music readable, there are several rules. We need not worry about these yet, but you will often see two notes tied together instead of one long one.

SCALES &
ACCIDENTALS

INTERVALS
& CHORDS

ARPEGGIOS

EXPRESSION

FURTHER
TECHNIQUES

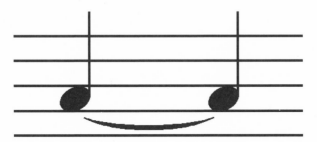

FREE ACCESS on iPhone & Android
etc, using any free QR code app

Scan to **HEAR** chords and scales, or
go directly to flametreemusic.com

For very, very long notes (spanning several bars) we can chain all the notes together using ties.

There is no limit to how many notes can be tied together. Just play the first note and hold it down for the combined length of all the notes.

For example, a **half note (minim)** tied to a **quarter note (crotchet)** will last for 3 beats (2 plus 1).

You will never see rests tied together – only notes.

Try this exercise which makes use of ties.

My Bow Tie

START
HERE

ALL THE
BASICS

**RHYTHM
& NOTES**

SCALES &
ACCIDENTALS

INTERVALS
& CHORDS

ARPEGGIOS

EXPRESSION

FURTHER
TECHNIQUES

Dotted Notes

Another way of increasing the length of a note is to add a dot to it.

A dot has a specific length in relation to the note it is placed after. It lasts for half the length of the note. Therefore a **dot** placed **after** a **half note (minim)**, which would normally last for two beats, will **increase** the length to three beats.

All the equivalent rests can also have dots placed after them, so a dotted half note rest (dotted minim rest) will be 3 beats of silence.

Opposite are some notes both with and without dots, so you can see the lengths.

START HERE

ALL THE BASICS

RHYTHM & NOTES

SCALES & ACCIDENTALS

INTERVALS & CHORDS

ARPEGGIOS

EXPRESSION

FURTHER TECHNIQUES

Note	Length	Dotted Note	Length
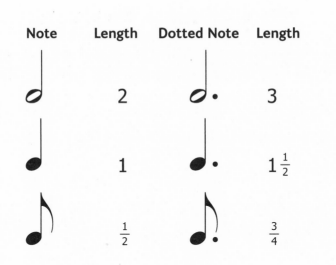	2		3
	1		$1\frac{1}{2}$
	$\frac{1}{2}$		$\frac{3}{4}$

Try this exercise which makes use of dotted notes.

Spotty Dotty

START
HERE

ALL THE
BASICS

**RHYTHM
& NOTES**

SCALES &
ACCIDENTALS

INTERVALS
& CHORDS

ARPEGGIOS

EXPRESSION

FURTHER
TECHNIQUES

Time Signatures

So far we have been using bars with four beats in. This need not be the case for all tunes. Music can be in one of several time signatures.

A time signature consists of two numbers.

- The **top** number tells you how many beats there are in each bar.

- The **bottom** number tells you what sort of beat to use:

    - a **2** stands for **half notes (minims)**

    - a **4** stands for **quarter notes (crotchets)**

    - an **8** stands for **eighth notes (quavers)**.

All the music we have been playing so far has been four quarter notes (crotchets) in each bar – this time signature will have a figure 4 on the top and a 4 on the bottom.

The following pages introduce four of the most common time signatures:

$$\frac{4}{4} \qquad \frac{3}{4} \qquad \frac{2}{4} \qquad \frac{6}{8}$$

START HERE

ALL THE BASICS

RHYTHM & NOTES

SCALES & ACCIDENTALS

INTERVALS & CHORDS

ARPEGGIOS

EXPRESSION

FURTHER TECHNIQUES

START
HERE

ALL THE
BASICS

RHYTHM
& NOTES

SCALES &
ACCIDENTALS

INTERVALS
& CHORDS

ARPEGGIOS

EXPRESSION

FURTHER
TECHNIQUES

FREE ACCESS on iPhone & Android
etc, using any free QR code app

Scan to **HEAR** chords and scales, or
go directly to flametreemusic.com

Four quarter notes (crotchets) per bar.

Here is a bar filled with quarter notes (crotchets):

Now try this tune in 4/4 which uses several different note types.

Round About 4

3/4

Three quarter notes (crotchets) per bar.

Here is a bar filled with quarter notes (crotchets):

Now try this tune in 3/4 which uses several different note types.

Three For Tea

Scan to **HEAR** chords and scales, or go directly to flametreemusic.com

START HERE

ALL THE BASICS

RHYTHM & NOTES

SCALES & ACCIDENTALS

INTERVALS & CHORDS

ARPEGGIOS

EXPRESSION

FURTHER TECHNIQUES

Two quarter notes (crotchets) per bar.

Here is a bar filled with quarter notes (crotchets):

Now try this tune in 2/4 which uses several different note types:

Two's Company

FREE ACCESS on iPhone & Android etc, using any free QR code app

Scan to **HEAR** chords and scales, or go directly to flametreemusic.com

6/8

Six eighth notes (quavers) per bar.

Below is a bar with eighth notes (quavers). See that in 6/8 the eighth notes (quavers) are grouped in threes.

Now try this tune in 6/8 which uses several different note types. Dotted quarter notes (crotchets) are common in 6/8.

Run Around Six

Scan to **HEAR** chords and scales, or go directly to flametreemusic.com

START HERE

ALL THE BASICS

RHYTHM & NOTES

SCALES & ACCIDENTALS

INTERVALS & CHORDS

ARPEGGIOS

EXPRESSION

FURTHER TECHNIQUES

What We Know So Far

This section has been all about rhythm.

1. Rhythm is all about the relationship of notes to a regular **pulse**.

2. Different note types have different **lengths**, and every note has an equivalent rest.

3. Both notes and rests can increase their length by half with a **dot** placed after the note or rest.

4. Notes can also be made longer by **tying** together two or more notes.

5. **Time signatures** tell you how many **beats** are in each bar, and what sort of beat they are.

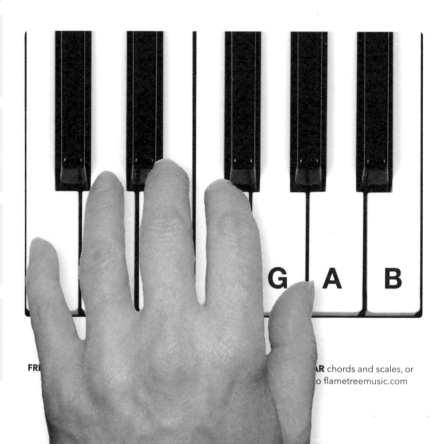

G A B

FR... ...R chords and scales, or
...o flametreemusic.com

Now Try This

The tunes on the next pages pull together all you have learned in this section.

1. Remember to keep a **steady pulse** all the way through.

2. You will find that putting a little **emphasis** on the **first note** in **every bar** will help you keep a steady rhythm.

3. Do not play too fast – it is more important to **keep a steady pulse**.

4. **The left hand** in some of these exercises is **used** to help **keep** the **rhythm steady** – with notes just on the main beats of the bar, which are usually the first beat and sometimes the middle beat of each bar.

5. **Practise each tune hands separately** at first so you can see what each hand is doing, then try putting the hands together.

6. **Use a metronome** to help you keep the pulse steady – a setting between 60 and 80 will work well for these tunes.

START
HERE

ALL THE
BASICS

RHYTHM
& NOTES

SCALES &
ACCIDENTALS

INTERVALS
& CHORDS

ARPEGGIOS

EXPRESSION

FURTHER
TECHNIQUES

FREE ACCESS on iPhone & Android etc, using any free QR code app

Scan to **HEAR** chords and scales, or go directly to flametreemusic.com

Three Blind Mice

Tea Pot Twirl

FREE ACCESS on iPhone & Android
etc, using any free QR code app

Scan to **HEAR** chords and scales, or
go directly to flametreemusic.com

START
HERE

ALL THE
BASICS

RHYTHM
& NOTES

SCALES &
ACCIDENTALS

INTERVALS
& CHORDS

ARPEGGIOS

EXPRESSION

FURTHER
TECHNIQUES

This Old Man

START
HERE

ALL THE
BASICS

RHYTHM
& NOTES

SCALES &
ACCIDENTALS

INTERVALS
& CHORDS

ARPEGGIOS

EXPRESSION

FURTHER
TECHNIQUES

Mitzi's Waltz

Royal Tune

**START
HERE**

**ALL THE
BASICS**

**RHYTHM
& NOTES**

**SCALES &
ACCIDENTALS**

**INTERVALS
& CHORDS**

ARPEGGIOS

EXPRESSION

**FURTHER
TECHNIQUES**

FREE ACCESS on iPhone & Android
etc, using any free QR code app

Scan to **HEAR** chords and scales, or
go directly to flametreemusic.com

Syncopated Twos

Copy Cat Bounce

Scan to **HEAR** chords and scales, or
go directly to flametreemusic.com

START HERE

ALL THE BASICS

RHYTHM & NOTES

SCALES & ACCIDENTALS

INTERVALS & CHORDS

ARPEGGIOS

EXPRESSION

FURTHER TECHNIQUES

Hands Together

Before we get in to adding sharps and flats, it would be a good idea to practise playing with the hands together. The left hand is sometimes used to accompany the tune in the right hand and sometimes it has tunes of its own.

On this page you will see a reminder about which finger has which number. The tunes that follow will have some fingering on them to help you put your hand in the correct place.

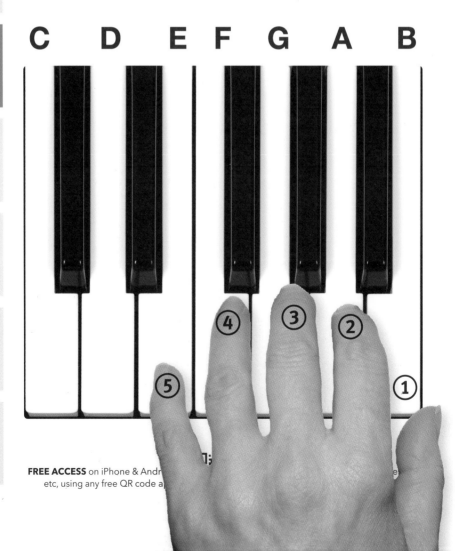

As always with hands-together music, you should learn each hand on its own first. The tunes will not involve moving the hands too often and too far, but we will get more adventurous as we progress.

The following four tunes have all been adapted from piano pieces by Wolfgang Amadeus Mozart, a renowned Classical composer who lived during the second half of the eighteenth century. Practise playing all four pieces, to get used to playing with both hands.

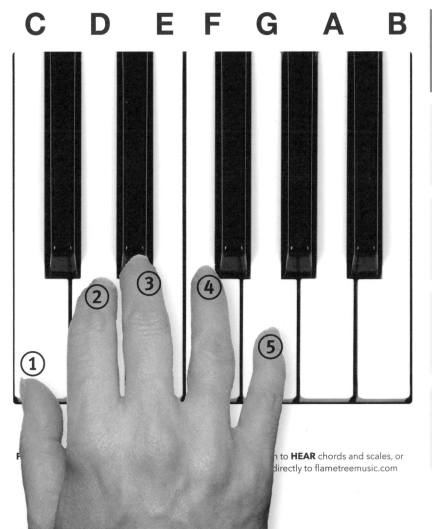

...h to **HEAR** chords and scales, or ...directly to flametreemusic.com

START HERE

ALL THE BASICS

RHYTHM & NOTES

SCALES &
ACCIDENTALS

INTERVALS & CHORDS

ARPEGGIOS

EXPRESSION

FURTHER TECHNIQUES

Twinkle Twinkle

Rondo

FREE ACCESS on iPhone & Android
etc, using any free QR code app

Scan to **HEAR** chords and scales, or
go directly to flametreemusic.com

START
HERE

ALL THE
BASICS

RHYTHM
& NOTES

SCALES &
ACCIDENTALS

INTERVALS
& CHORDS

ARPEGGIOS

EXPRESSION

FURTHER
TECHNIQUES

Allegro 1

Allegro 2

START
HERE

ALL THE
BASICS

RHYTHM
& NOTES

SCALES &
ACCIDENTALS

INTERVALS
& CHORDS

ARPEGGIOS

EXPRESSION

FURTHER
TECHNIQUES

Key Signatures

Key signature is the name given to the collection of sharps or flats at the start of the music. A key signature will consist of just sharps or just flats, you will not get a mixture of both.

Every note on the piano has a **sharp** and a **flat** version, but we will only concern ourselves with key signatures of just one or two sharps or flats for this section.

If there are **no sharps** or **flats** at the start of the music then this too is a key signature – it is the key signature of **C major** and **A minor**.

All the tunes you have played so far have had a C major key signature.

Tunes in C major just use the white notes on the piano – we are now going to venture into using **black notes** in our tunes.

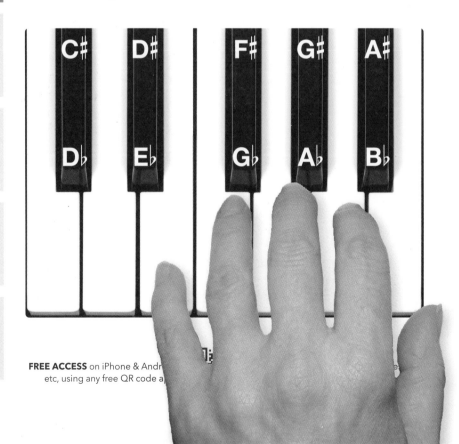

START
HERE

ALL THE
BASICS

RHYTHM
& NOTES

SCALES &
ACCIDENTALS

INTERVALS
& CHORDS

ARPEGGIOS

EXPRESSION

FURTHER
TECHNIQUES

START HERE

ALL THE BASICS

RHYTHM & NOTES

SCALES & ACCIDENTALS

INTERVALS & CHORDS

ARPEGGIOS

EXPRESSION

FURTHER TECHNIQUES

FREE ACCESS on iPhone & Android etc, using any free QR code app

Scan to **HEAR** chords and scales, or go directly to flametreemusic.com

G major

This is a G major key signature.

It has one sharp:
F sharp.

D major

This is a D major key signature.

It has two sharps:
F sharp and **C sharp.**

FREE ACCESS on iPhone & Android
etc, using any free QR code app

Scan to **HEAR** chords and scales, or
go directly to flametreemusic.com

START HERE

ALL THE BASICS

RHYTHM & NOTES

SCALES & ACCIDENTALS

INTERVALS & CHORDS

ARPEGGIOS

EXPRESSION

FURTHER TECHNIQUES

F major

This is an F major key signature.

It has one flat:
B flat.

B flat major

This is a B flat major key signature.

It has two flats:
B flat and **E flat**.

On the next page there are some tunes using our new key signatures.

FREE ACCESS on iPhone & Android
etc, using any free QR code app

Scan to **HEAR** chords and scales, or
go directly to flametreemusic.com

SCALES & ACCIDENTALS

Waltz in G

D Major Bounce

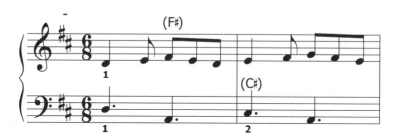

FREE ACCESS on iPhone & Android
etc, using any free QR code app

Scan to **HEAR** chords and scales, or
go directly to flametreemusic.com

START
HERE

ALL THE
BASICS

RHYTHM
& NOTES

SCALES &
ACCIDENTALS

INTERVALS
& CHORDS

ARPEGGIOS

EXPRESSION

FURTHER
TECHNIQUES

Fun in F

B Flat Ballad

START
HERE

ALL THE
BASICS

RHYTHM
& NOTES

SCALES &
ACCIDENTALS

INTERVALS
& CHORDS

ARPEGGIOS

EXPRESSION

FURTHER
TECHNIQUES

FREE ACCESS on iPhone & Android etc, using any free QR code app

Scan to **HEAR** chords and scales, or go directly to flametreemusic.com

Accidentals

Sometimes we need to make a note sharp or flat temporarily. This is where accidentals come in.

If you put an **accidental** sharp in **front** of **a note**, that note will change to a sharp and will stay as a sharp for the rest of the bar. As soon as you get to the **next bar** the note will **revert** back to what it was.

Accidentals can be **sharp**, **flat** or **natural**.

A **sharp** will change a note to the next note **higher** (usually a black note) and a **flat** will change it to the next note **lower**.

A **natural converts** a sharp or flat **back** to the respective white note – you will generally come across naturals when you have music in key signatures with sharps and flats in.

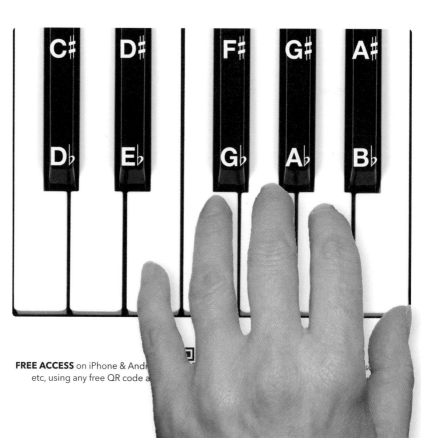

FREE ACCESS on iPhone & Andr___ etc, using any free QR code a___

Sharp

This is a sharp sign.

It means play the very next note to the right,
which is usually a black note.

The notes E and B do not have black notes to the
right of them, so their sharps are white notes.

START
HERE

ALL THE
BASICS

RHYTHM
& NOTES

SCALES &
ACCIDENTALS

INTERVALS
& CHORDS

ARPEGGIOS

EXPRESSION

FURTHER
TECHNIQUES

FREE ACCESS on iPhone & Android
etc, using any free QR code app

Scan to **HEAR** chords and scales, or
go directly to flametreemusic.com

Flat

This is a flat sign.

**It means play the very next note to the left,
which is usually a black note.**

**The notes F and C do not have black notes to
the left of them, so their flats are white notes.**

START
HERE

ALL THE
BASICS

RHYTHM
& NOTES

**SCALES &
ACCIDENTALS**

INTERVALS
& CHORDS

ARPEGGIOS

EXPRESSION

FURTHER
TECHNIQUES

FREE ACCESS on iPhone & Android
etc, using any free QR code app

Scan to **HEAR** chords and scales, or
go directly to flametreemusic.com

Natural

This is a natural sign.

It is used to cancel a sharp or flat.

Just play the white note.

START
HERE

ALL THE
BASICS

RHYTHM
& NOTES

SCALES &
ACCIDENTALS

INTERVALS
& CHORDS

ARPEGGIOS

EXPRESSION

FURTHER
TECHNIQUES

Simple Major Scales

You will come across scales, or parts of scales, in many pieces of music.

Look out for rows of notes either going up or going down.

On the opposite page a **C major scale** is shown in both hands, first going up, then going down. Look at the fingering suggested – this makes it easier to play smoothly. (As a reminder, the scale, which uses the white notes only, is also shown below.)

When you need to play the thumb after finger 3, tuck the thumb under to play the next note without a gap. Then, when you are going the other way and need to play '3' after '1', lift finger 3 over the top of the thumb.

Try the tunes on the following pages, all of which include some scale-like passages. See how many scales you can recognize – the first few are pointed out for you.

START HERE

ALL THE BASICS

RHYTHM & NOTES

SCALES & ACCIDENTALS

INTERVALS & CHORDS

ARPEGGIOS

EXPRESSION

FURTHER TECHNIQUES

C D E F G A B

FREE ACCESS on iPhone & Android etc, using any free QR code app

Scan to **HEAR** chords and scales, or go directly to flametreemusic.com

C major scale, going up

Right hand

Left hand

C major scale, going down

Right hand

Left hand

Scan to **HEAR** chords and scales, or go directly to flametreemusic.com

START HERE

ALL THE BASICS

RHYTHM & NOTES

SCALES & ACCIDENTALS

INTERVALS & CHORDS

ARPEGGIOS

EXPRESSION

FURTHER TECHNIQUES

Little Nut Tree

Chiming Bells

FREE ACCESS on iPhone & Android
etc, using any free QR code app

Scan to **HEAR** chords and scales, or
go directly to flametreemusic.com

START
HERE

ALL THE
BASICS

RHYTHM
& NOTES

SCALES &
ACCIDENTALS

INTERVALS
& CHORDS

ARPEGGIOS

EXPRESSION

FURTHER
TECHNIQUES

Polly Put The Kettle On

START
HERE

ALL THE
BASICS

RHYTHM
& NOTES

SCALES &
ACCIDENTALS

INTERVALS
& CHORDS

ARPEGGIOS

EXPRESSION

FURTHER
TECHNIQUES

FREE ACCESS on iPhone & Android etc, using any free QR code app

Scan to **HEAR** chords and scales, or go directly to flametreemusic.com

Playing By Ear

Remember we learned about playing by ear earlier in the book? You need to listen and create musical shapes in your head.

Here are two tunes with bits missing – try to fill in the gaps with scale-like passages.

You can either copy the shape of the bar before, or mirror what you are given.

You could even play something completely different – as long as it sounds like it fits in with the rest of the music.

Listen carefully to the sound – you may need a few sharps and flats to make it sound right!

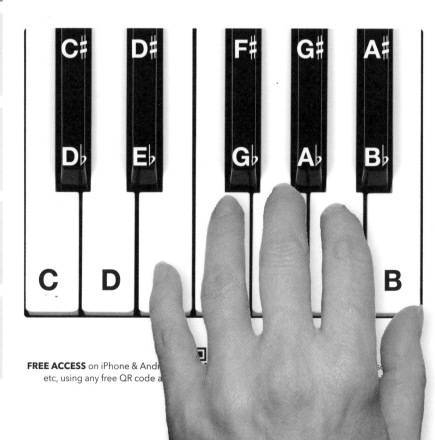

FREE ACCESS on iPhone & Andr... ...
etc, using any free QR code a...

Fill The Gap 1

Fill The Gap 2

START
HERE

ALL THE
BASICS

RHYTHM
& NOTES

SCALES &
ACCIDENTALS

INTERVALS
& CHORDS

ARPEGGIOS

EXPRESSION

FURTHER
TECHNIQUES

FREE ACCESS on iPhone & Android
etc, using any free QR code app

Scan to **HEAR** chords and scales, or
go directly to flametreemusic.com

START
HERE

ALL THE
BASICS

RHYTHM
& NOTES

SCALES &
ACCIDENTALS

INTERVALS
& CHORDS

ARPEGGIOS

EXPRESSION

FURTHER
TECHNIQUES

What We Know So Far

This section has been all about moving away from just playing the white notes.

1. You have learned all about **sharps**, **flats** and **naturals** – when sharps and flats are collected together at the beginning of the music they are called a **key signature**.

2. Sharps, flats and naturals in front of individual notes are called **accidentals**.

3. Every key signature has a **major scale** and a **minor scale** associated with it. We have learned a few basic ones so far – there are more to come later in the book.

4. Many tunes have **scale-like passages** in them. If you know your scales you will automatically have learned part of almost every tune you will want to play.

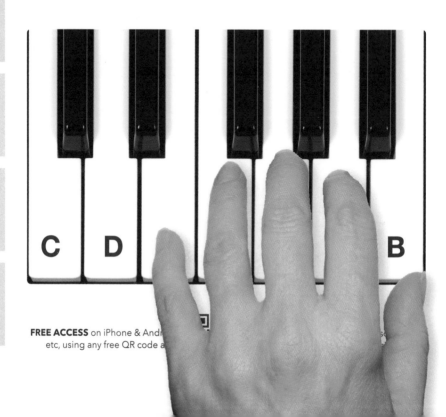

C   D   B

FREE ACCESS on iPhone & Andr...
etc, using any free QR code a...

Now Try This

The next two pages combine what we have learned in this section. They are tunes from famous composers which include parts of scales and many other things you have just learned. These tunes also allow you to practise playing in different keys.

Some things to look out for:

Key signature at the start of the music.

Part of a scale going upwards.

Part of a scale going downwards.

Accidentals in the music.

START HERE

ALL THE BASICS

RHYTHM & NOTES

SCALES & ACCIDENTALS

INTERVALS & CHORDS

ARPEGGIOS

EXPRESSION

FURTHER TECHNIQUES

FREE ACCESS on iPhone & Android etc, using any free QR code app

Scan to **HEAR** chords and scales, or go directly to flametreemusic.com

Melody (Schumann)

FREE ACCESS on iPhone & Android
etc, using any free QR code app

Scan to **HEAR** chords and scales, or
go directly to flametreemusic.com

Mazurka in C (Chopin)

* This note would be a natural anyway, but an accidental is often added when you have just played a sharp as a reminder.

START HERE

ALL THE BASICS

RHYTHM & NOTES

SCALES & ACCIDENTALS

INTERVALS & CHORDS

ARPEGGIOS

EXPRESSION

FURTHER TECHNIQUES

Intervals

An interval is the distance between two notes. You count the lowest notes as '1' then count up through the letter names until you reach the higher note.

The easiest way to see how this works is to use the **C major scale** and see how far each note of the scale is from the starting note.

C to D is just 1 step,

so C = 1 then D = 2.

It is called a second.

C to E is two steps up,

so C = 1, D = 2 and E = 3.

It is called a third.

Look at the chart opposite. This shows you all the main intervals in the keys of **C major** and **G major**.

FREE ACCESS on iPhone & Android etc, using any free QR code app

Scan to **HEAR** chords and scales, or go directly to flametreemusic.com

START HERE

ALL THE BASICS

RHYTHM & NOTES

SCALES & ACCIDENTALS

INTERVALS & CHORDS

ARPEGGIOS

EXPRESSION

FURTHER TECHNIQUES

Intervals in C major

Right Hand

2nd   3rd   4th   5th   6th   7th Octave

Left Hand

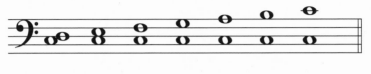

2nd   3rd   4th   5th   6th   7th Octave

Intervals in G major

Right Hand

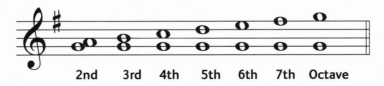

2nd   3rd   4th   5th   6th   7th Octave

Left Hand

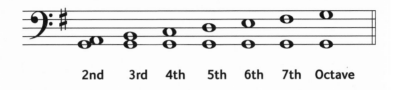

2nd   3rd   4th   5th   6th   7th Octave

START HERE

ALL THE BASICS

RHYTHM & NOTES

SCALES & ACCIDENTALS

INTERVALS & CHORDS

ARPEGGIOS

EXPRESSION

FURTHER TECHNIQUES

FREE ACCESS on iPhone & Android etc, using any free QR code app

Scan to **HEAR** chords and scales, or go directly to flametreemusic.com

START
HERE

ALL THE
BASICS

RHYTHM
& NOTES

SCALES &
ACCIDENTALS

INTERVALS
& CHORDS

ARPEGGIOS

EXPRESSION

FURTHER
TECHNIQUES

Exercises

Here are a few exercises using intervals.

Intervals can be written with the notes clustered together (known as a **harmonic interval**) or with the notes played one after the other (known as a **melodic interval**).

These exercises use both – look carefully and you will see the difference between harmonic intervals and melodic intervals.

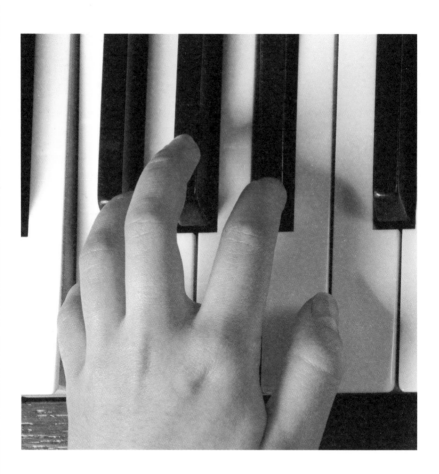

FREE ACCESS on iPhone & Android
etc, using any free QR code app

Scan to **HEAR** chords and scales, or
go directly to flametreemusic.com

Jumping in Three

Chorale (Schumann)

START
HERE

ALL THE
BASICS

RHYTHM
& NOTES

SCALES &
ACCIDENTALS

INTERVALS
& CHORDS

ARPEGGIOS

EXPRESSION

FURTHER
TECHNIQUES

FREE ACCESS on iPhone & Android
etc, using any free QR code app

Scan to **HEAR** chords and scales, or
go directly to flametreemusic.com

Simple Chords

Here are some simple 3-note chords, based just on the white notes.

Listen carefully and see if you can hear the **difference** between **major** and **minor** chords – generally, **major** chords are **brighter** and **minor** chords sound more **solemn**.

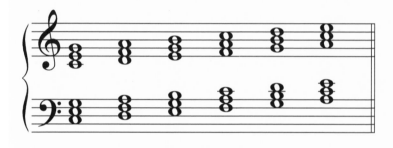

	C	D	E	F	G	A
	major	minor	minor	major	major	minor

The **chords** so far have been in '**root**' position.

This means that the **lowest note** of the chord is the one which gives it its name, so **C major** starts on its root note C, **G major** starts on its root G and **A minor** starts on the root note A.

FREE ACCESS on iPhone & Android etc, using any free QR code app

Scan to **HEAR** chords and scales, or go directly to flametreemusic.com

START
HERE

ALL THE
BASICS

RHYTHM
& NOTES

SCALES &
ACCIDENTALS

INTERVALS
& CHORDS

ARPEGGIOS

EXPRESSION

FURTHER
TECHNIQUES

We can play the same notes in a different order to get '**inverted**' chords.

Here are a few:

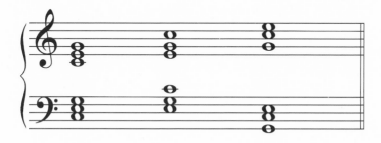

Root   **1st inversion**   **2nd inversion**

The next two pages have some simple chord exercises so you can get used to playing them.

START
HERE

ALL THE
BASICS

RHYTHM
& NOTES

SCALES &
ACCIDENTALS

**INTERVALS
& CHORDS**

ARPEGGIOS

EXPRESSION

FURTHER
TECHNIQUES

FREE ACCESS on iPhone & Android
etc, using any free QR code app

Scan to **HEAR** chords and scales, or
go directly to flametreemusic.com

Chords 1

Chords 2

FREE ACCESS on iPhone & Android
etc, using any free QR code app

Scan to **HEAR** chords and scales, or
go directly to flametreemusic.com

Chords 3

Chords 4

START
HERE

ALL THE
BASICS

RHYTHM
& NOTES

SCALES &
ACCIDENTALS

INTERVALS
& CHORDS

ARPEGGIOS

EXPRESSION

FURTHER
TECHNIQUES

Here are two simple tunes with just the **right hand** written out. Listen carefully to the music then try to **add** some **simple chords** in the **left hand** (one per bar).

Keep to 'root position' chords to begin with as these are easier to play. Remember to include sharps or flats if they are shown in the key signature.

The tunes which follow these are based on **intervals** and **chords**.

By the way, do you remember seeing and playing middle C**? It was pointed out quite early on in this book. If you look at the note you will see it has a little line of its own – this is called a ledger line. When you need notes higher or lower than would fit on the staff, you use** ledger lines**. Here are a few notes on ledger lines:**

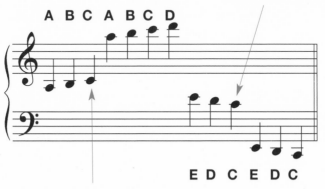

middle C on bass clef

middle C on treble clef

START
HERE

ALL THE
BASICS

RHYTHM
& NOTES

SCALES &
ACCIDENTALS

INTERVALS
& CHORDS

ARPEGGIOS

EXPRESSION

FURTHER
TECHNIQUES

FREE ACCESS on iPhone & Android
etc, using any free QR code app

Scan to **HEAR** chords and scales, or
go directly to flametreemusic.com

Dynamics

The word 'dynamics' means the louds and softs when playing the keys.

All the **main musical terms** you will come across in this section are **Italian** words – but don't worry, there are not too many of them.

The chart on the opposite page shows all the common dynamic markings. You will not often come across anything else.

We will follow this with some tunes that include dynamics so you can see how they look in the music.

START HERE

ALL THE BASICS

RHYTHM & NOTES

SCALES & ACCIDENTALS

INTERVALS & CHORDS

ARPEGGIOS

EXPRESSION

FURTHER TECHNIQUES

Symbol	Full Term	Meaning
ff	*fortissimo*	very loud
f	*forte*	loud
mf	*mezzoforte*	moderately loud
mp	*mezzopiano*	moderately soft
p	*piano*	soft
pp	*pianissimo*	very soft
<	*crescendo*	gradually louder
>	*decrescendo*	gradually softer

START HERE

ALL THE BASICS

RHYTHM & NOTES

SCALES & ACCIDENTALS

INTERVALS & CHORDS

ARPEGGIOS

EXPRESSION

FURTHER TECHNIQUES

FREE ACCESS on iPhone & Android etc, using any free QR code app

Scan to **HEAR** chords and scales, or go directly to flametreemusic.com

La Donna e Mobile (Verdi)

FREE ACCESS on iPhone & Android
etc, using any free QR code app

Scan to **HEAR** chords and scales, or
go directly to flametreemusic.com

START
HERE

ALL THE
BASICS

RHYTHM
& NOTES

SCALES &
ACCIDENTALS

INTERVALS
& CHORDS

ARPEGGIOS

EXPRESSION

FURTHER
TECHNIQUES

Minuet in G (Böhm)

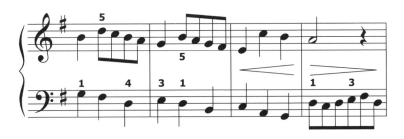

START HERE

ALL THE BASICS

RHYTHM & NOTES

SCALES & ACCIDENTALS

INTERVALS & CHORDS

ARPEGGIOS

EXPRESSION

FURTHER TECHNIQUES

Slurs

Curved lines are used in many places in a piece of music, and they can mean different things. You met one of these a while ago – that was the tie. A tie is a curved line joining two notes of the same pitch.

The curved line we are looking at here is one which **joins** two **different notes**, or it could go across three or more notes. A **slur**, in piano music, means **play** the **notes smoothly** (do not put a gap between the notes).

Here are some examples to show you the **difference** between **ties** and **slurs**. These are followed by some simple tunes with slurs included – make sure there are no gaps during each slur.

These are ties

These are slurs

FREE ACCESS on iPhone & Android etc, using any free QR code app

Scan to **HEAR** chords and scales, or go directly to flametreemusic.com

Bow The Lament

Slur's The Word

Staccato and Legato

In music, the opposite of smooth is 'detached'.

We have just learned about slurs, which show where to play smoothly, so now we need to know when to play detached – also called '**staccato**'.

There is a difference between 'leaving a gap' and playing 'staccato' – staccato is usually shorter.

Going back to the slur for a moment – there is another way for a composer to indicate smooth music. If a **whole section** is to be **smooth** and **without gaps** then the term used is '**legato**' – this saves having to put a slur line over everything.

The following exercises demonstrate the **difference** between separate, **legato** and **staccato**. When you understand this, play the tunes on the next page – there is one 'legato' tune and one 'staccato' tune.

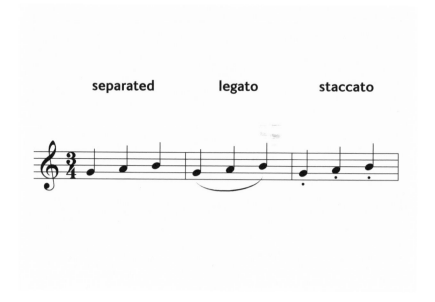

separated   legato   staccato

FREE ACCESS on iPhone & Android
etc, using any free QR code app

Scan to **HEAR** chords and scales, or
go directly to flametreemusic.com

START HERE

ALL THE BASICS

RHYTHM & NOTES

SCALES & ACCIDENTALS

INTERVALS & CHORDS

ARPEGGIOS

EXPRESSION

FURTHER TECHNIQUES

Minuet in G (Beethoven)

Scan to **HEAR** chords and scales, or
go directly to flametreemusic.com

Using Pedals

Most upright pianos have two pedals and most grand pianos have three. We will not worry about the middle pedal for now.

The pedal on the **left** is the **damping pedal** (often called the '**soft pedal**'), and the pedal on the **right** is called the '**sustaining pedal**'.

The **soft pedal** can physically work in a number of different ways, depending on how the piano is manufactured. Here are the three most common ways:

1. The hammers are moved closer to the strings, so they hit them with less force.

2. The hammers are all moved to the right so that notes with multiple strings just use one of them.

3. A piece of felt is raised between the hammers and the string, creating a muted sound.

Look inside your piano and press the pedal to see which technique yours uses.

The **sustaining pedal** simply **raises** the piano's **dampers off** the **strings** to allow any notes played to keep on sounding until they die out.

START HERE

ALL THE BASICS

RHYTHM & NOTES

SCALES & ACCIDENTALS

INTERVALS & CHORDS

ARPEGGIOS

EXPRESSION

FURTHER TECHNIQUES

START
HERE

ALL THE
BASICS

RHYTHM
& NOTES

SCALES &
ACCIDENTALS

INTERVALS
& CHORDS

ARPEGGIOS

EXPRESSION

FURTHER
TECHNIQUES

**Soft
Pedal**

**Sostenuto
Pedal**

**Sustain
Pedal**

FREE ACCESS on iPhone & Android
etc, using any free QR code app

Scan to **HEAR** chords and scales, or
go directly to flametreemusic.com

The Soft Pedal

The pedal on the left will not automatically make your music soft – you can still play loud with this pedal depressed.

What it does is make it a lot easier to play softly, and will allow you to play much softer than without it.

Try the following tune both with and without the soft pedal – see how quietly you can play without the notes disappearing completely.

Quietly Does It

START HERE

ALL THE BASICS

RHYTHM & NOTES

SCALES & ACCIDENTALS

INTERVALS & CHORDS

ARPEGGIOS

EXPRESSION

FURTHER TECHNIQUES

The Sustaining Pedal

The marking in the music which tells you to press this pedal is either a simple 'P' or a swirly 'Ped.' symbol.

Release the pedal where you see a star. Sometimes the duration of the pedal is marked with a horizontal line – the vertical line at the end shows where to release the pedal.

The next tune is shown using both methods so you can see them in context.

START
HERE

ALL THE
BASICS

RHYTHM
& NOTES

SCALES &
ACCIDENTALS

INTERVALS
& CHORDS

ARPEGGIOS

EXPRESSION

FURTHER
TECHNIQUES

Long, Long Ago

Right Hand Technique

There are many ways to improve your playing, both to make it sound better and to make it easier on the hands. This is where technique comes in.

Here are some reminders of the most important points:

1. Keep your **hand relaxed** (not tense).
2. **Fingers** should be **gently curved**.
3. Your **arm** should feel like it is **floating** along.

When you need to play fast, it is vital to stay relaxed as if you let your hand get tense this will slow the muscles down.

1. For **fast runs** of notes, try to **keep your hand steady** and let your fingers do the work.
2. For **trills** (quick alternation between two notes) let your **hand rock a little**.
3. For lots of **staccato**, let your **wrist** help – don't try to just use the fingers.

The next tune makes use of fast runs and trills.

START HERE

ALL THE BASICS

RHYTHM & NOTES

SCALES & ACCIDENTALS

INTERVALS & CHORDS

ARPEGGIOS

EXPRESSION

FURTHER TECHNIQUES

Allegro in D (Steinberger)

What We Know So Far

In the earlier sections we learned about pitches and lengths, and we also learned about different ways of moving around the keyboard. This section has introduced the following:

1. **Dynamics** – music can be loud, soft or somewhere in between.

2. Letters, which stand for **Italian words**, **indicate** how **loud** or **soft** to **play**.

3. Notes can be smooth (**legato**) or detached (**staccato**).

4. **Legato** music can be indicated by a curved line called a **slur**.

5. **Staccato** notes are indicated with a **dot** above or below them.

6. The **left pedal** helps you play **quietly**.

7. The **right pedal sustains** the notes played.

8. **Good technique** will help you play better.

FREE ACCESS on iPhone & Android etc, using any free QR code app

Scan to **HEAR** chords and scales, or go directly to flametreemusic.com

START HERE

ALL THE BASICS

RHYTHM & NOTES

SCALES & ACCIDENTALS

INTERVALS & CHORDS

ARPEGGIOS

EXPRESSION

FURTHER TECHNIQUES

Find The Chords 1

Find The Chords 2

Scan to **HEAR** chords and scales, or go directly to flametreemusic.com

What We Know So Far

This chapter has been all about intervals and chords.

1. The distance between two notes is called an **interval**.

2. **The size of an interval is the** number of notes from the lowest to the highest, counting the starting note as 1.

3. Intervals can be played as **separate** notes one after the other or played **together**.

4. A **chord** is a group of notes played together.

5. The most common chords are either **major** or **minor**.

6. Chords are named after the **lowest** note, when played in **root** position.

7. **Chords** are a common way of **accompanying** a melody.

8. Not all instruments can play chords. A **piano** and a **guitar** can, but brass or wind instruments, such as a trumpet or clarinet, cannot.

FREE ACCESS on iPhone & Android etc, using any free QR code app

Scan to **HEAR** chords and scales, or go directly to flametreemusic.com

Now Try This

Music with intervals and chords

The music on the next few pages will help you practise playing chords. You can also go to the Flame Tree Red Book **in the** Pieces section **online at FlameTreeMusic.com, to find more sheet music.**

Sometimes a chord is not played with all the notes at once but one after the other. You have already met this type of accompaniment in previous sections. Look back at some of the pieces by Mozart you have played and see if you can spot the **'broken' chords**.

It is often the left hand that plays **chords**, but the right hand can play them as well. As you listen to music, decide whether it is a simple melody with a chordal accompaniment or both hands are playing chords.

There is a specific type of 'broken' chord called an **arpeggio**. We will learn about these soon.

START
HERE

ALL THE
BASICS

RHYTHM
& NOTES

SCALES &
ACCIDENTALS

INTERVALS
& CHORDS

ARPEGGIOS

EXPRESSION

FURTHER
TECHNIQUES

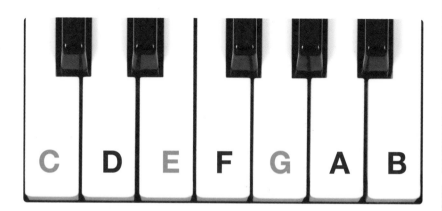

FREE ACCESS on iPhone & Android etc, using any free QR code app

Scan to **HEAR** chords and scales, or go directly to flametreemusic.com

Presto (Mozart)

Scan to **HEAR** chords and scales, or
go directly to flametreemusic.com

Presto (Haydn)

START
HERE

ALL THE
BASICS

RHYTHM
& NOTES

SCALES &
ACCIDENTALS

INTERVALS
& CHORDS

ARPEGGIOS

EXPRESSION

FURTHER
TECHNIQUES

FREE ACCESS on iPhone & Android
etc, using any free QR code app

Scan to **HEAR** chords and scales, or
go directly to flametreemusic.com

Moving Around The Keyboard

Scales help you move around the keyboard note by note, but broken chords and arpeggios help you move around in larger steps.

The exercises on the following two pages show you ways of moving around the keyboard using arpeggios. Take note of the fingering – as in the scales, the thumb should be tucked under the fingers to reach the next note to make all the notes smooth and avoid gaps in the sound.

Broken chords are also a very effective way of creating a moving accompaniment rather than a static one. Look back at some of the music you have just learned.

Here are some examples of broken chords:

Here's another note you need to know:

It is a sixteenth note (semiquaver). It is **half** the length of an **eighth note (quaver)**, so you will need 16 of them to fill a standard bar. Sixteenth notes are often written in groups of 4. Here is a 4/4 bar full of sixteenth notes.

START HERE

ALL THE BASICS

RHYTHM & NOTES

SCALES & ACCIDENTALS

INTERVALS & CHORDS

ARPEGGIOS

EXPRESSION

FURTHER TECHNIQUES

Scan to **HEAR** chords and scales, or go directly to flametreemusic.com

C major chord

3 note chord   4 note chord

Broken chord using 3 notes

Broken chord using 4 notes

Now try the exercises overleaf to practise arpeggios.

Arpeggio Exercise 1

Arpeggio Exercise 2

Arpeggio Melody

Simple Broken Chords

The word 'arpeggio' refers to a more formal playing of the broken chord in that all the notes of the chord should be played in order.

A broken chord is simply the notes of the chord 'broken up' into single notes played one after the other.

Here are two simple examples, one of a broken chord pattern and one of an arpeggio pattern. Both are based on the C major chord.

FREE ACCESS on iPhone & Android etc, using any free QR code app

Scan to **HEAR** chords and scales, or go directly to flametreemusic.com

Broken chord based on C major

C major arpeggio

START
HERE

ALL THE
BASICS

RHYTHM
& NOTES

SCALES &
ACCIDENTALS

INTERVALS
& CHORDS

ARPEGGIOS

EXPRESSION

FURTHER
TECHNIQUES

The two tunes that follow are basically the same, but the first uses broken chords and the second uses arpeggios.

You can try adding your own accompaniment instead. Use broken chords and arpeggios. There is just one chord per bar.

Waltz in G (broken chord version)

FREE ACCESS on iPhone & Android
etc, using any free QR code app

Scan to **HEAR** chords and scales, or
go directly to flametreemusic.com

Waltz in G (arpeggio chord version)

FREE ACCESS on iPhone & Android etc, using any free QR code app

Scan to **HEAR** chords and scales, or go directly to flametreemusic.com

What We Know So Far

This section has been all about broken chords and arpeggios. Here are a few things to remember:

1. **Broken chords** are **notes** of a **chord** played **one at a time**.

2. **Arpeggios** are **broken chords**, but with all the notes of the chord **played in order**.

3. **Broken chords** are a common way of creating an **accompaniment** to a tune.

4. **Broken chords** and **arpeggios** are an effective way of **moving around** the **keyboard** without jumping about.

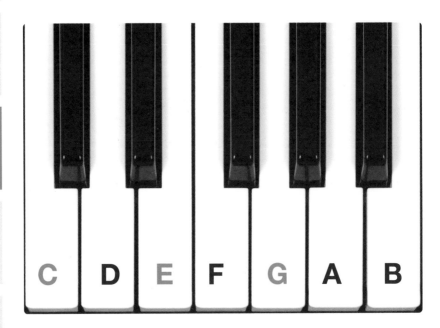

FREE ACCESS on iPhone & Android etc, using any free QR code app

Scan to **HEAR** chords and scales, or go directly to flametreemusic.com

Now Try This

What we need now are some examples of well-known music that uses broken chords and arpeggios.

The following pages contain music specially chosen to demonstrate this.

Don't forget, broken chords can appear in either hand and can be an accompaniment or an integral part of the melody.

Listen carefully as you play and see if you can spot all the broken chords.

Also see if you can work out what chord is actually being used. To do this, play the notes which you think are part of the broken chord all together.

START
HERE

ALL THE
BASICS

RHYTHM
& NOTES

SCALES &
ACCIDENTALS

INTERVALS
& CHORDS

ARPEGGIOS

EXPRESSION

FURTHER
TECHNIQUES

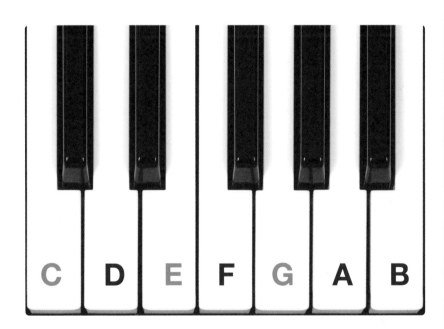

FREE ACCESS on iPhone & Android
etc, using any free QR code app

Scan to **HEAR** chords and scales, or
go directly to flametreemusic.com

Rondo in G (Bertini)

Now Try This

Let's put all these new ideas together. The music that follows has all the indications you would expect in a complete piece of music. These indications help you to play the music exactly as the composer intended.

Try playing some of these tunes completely ignoring all the dynamics and other markings. Then play them with everything included. Can you hear how much better the music sounds when you follow all the dynamics and other markings?

We will add just one more symbol – a shorthand way of writing quickly alternating notes. It is called a **trill**.

Notice that you need to fit in an extra note near the end (called the **turn**) in order for the trill to flow **smoothly** into the next note. The number of notes you can fit in will depend on the style and speed of the music.

This is what the **trill sign** looks like...

...and this is how you play it (the 5 signifies 5 notes should be played in the space of 4):

Scan to **HEAR** chords and scales, or go directly to flametreemusic.com

START HERE

ALL THE BASICS

RHYTHM & NOTES

SCALES & ACCIDENTALS

INTERVALS & CHORDS

ARPEGGIOS

EXPRESSION

FURTHER TECHNIQUES

The Merry Peasant (Schumann)

FREE ACCESS on iPhone & Android
etc, using any free QR code app

Scan to **HEAR** chords and scales, or
go directly to flametreemusic.com

German Dance (Weber)

START
HERE

ALL THE
BASICS

RHYTHM
& NOTES

SCALES &
ACCIDENTALS

INTERVALS
& CHORDS

ARPEGGIOS

EXPRESSION

FURTHER
TECHNIQUES

More Key Signatures

So far we have used up to two sharps or two flats in key signatures. We will now add key signatures with up to five sharps or flats.

As mentioned when key signatures were first introduced, they can indicate either a major or minor key. The minor key (known as the '**relative minor**') for a particular key signature can be found by **counting down three half steps (semitones)** from the **major key**. A 'half step' is the distance from one note to the very next one, irrespective of whether it is black or white. So the relative minor of C major is A minor.

The chart below shows all the key signatures with up to five sharps or flats and indicates both the major and minor names. We will follow this with a tune using one of the new key signatures.

Key Signatures up to five sharps/flats

A major / F# minor

B♭ major / G minor

C major / A minor

E major / C# minor

E♭ major / C minor

G major / E minor

B major / G# minor

A♭ major / F minor

D major / B minor

F major / D minor

D♭ major / B♭ minor

START HERE

ALL THE BASICS

RHYTHM & NOTES

SCALES & ACCIDENTALS

INTERVALS & CHORDS

ARPEGGIOS

EXPRESSION

FURTHER TECHNIQUES

Finale from Sonata in A (Haydn)

START
HERE

ALL THE
BASICS

RHYTHM
& NOTES

SCALES &
ACCIDENTALS

INTERVALS
& CHORDS

ARPEGGIOS

EXPRESSION

FURTHER
TECHNIQUES

FREE ACCESS on iPhone & Android
etc, using any free QR code app

Scan to **HEAR** chords and scales, or
go directly to flametreemusic.com

Harmonic Minor Scales

Major scales are pretty straightforward to play – you just play all the notes from the root note, over one octave, making notes sharp or flat according to the key signature.

Minor scales are slightly different in that you need to make a small adjustment to the notes. Don't worry – it is the same change for all keys.

In the **harmonic minor scale**, you start on the root note – but when you get to the **seventh note** you need to **sharpen it**. If the note starts off as a white note then that is easy, but if it is a flat then you need to remember that it will become a natural (to sharpen a note you move it one to the right).

Look at the examples opposite and you will see.

There are just a few additional time signatures and symbols to learn, which will increase the range of music you can play.

3 quavers per bar	9 quavers per bar	12 quavers per bar	2 minims per bar

FURTHER
TECHNIQUES

A harmonic minor

sharpened 7th

D harmonic minor

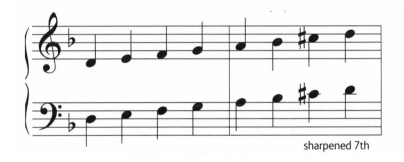

sharpened 7th

B flat harmonic minor

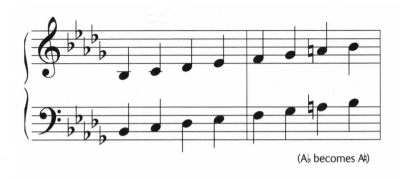

(A♭ becomes A♮)

START HERE

ALL THE BASICS

RHYTHM & NOTES

SCALES & ACCIDENTALS

INTERVALS & CHORDS

ARPEGGIOS

EXPRESSION

FURTHER TECHNIQUES

Chromatic Scales

The final type of scale we will introduce is the chromatic scale.

The chromatic scale is basically **every note** within an **octave**, black and white.

Here is a chromatic scale:

Chromatic Scale on C

Opposite are two exercises to practise chromatic passages.

Also, the Red Book in the **pieces section** of **flametreemusic.com** includes tunes, with minor scales and chromatic scales – see if you can spot them.

Opposite are two exercises to practise chromatic passages.

Sidebar navigation:
START HERE
ALL THE BASICS
RHYTHM & NOTES
SCALES & ACCIDENTALS
INTERVALS & CHORDS
ARPEGGIOS
EXPRESSION
FURTHER TECHNIQUES

Chromatic Exercise 1

Chromatic Exercise 2

FREE ACCESS on iPhone & Android
etc, using any free QR code app

Scan to **HEAR** chords and scales, or
go directly to flametreemusic.com

START
HERE

ALL THE
BASICS

RHYTHM
& NOTES

SCALES &
ACCIDENTALS

INTERVALS
& CHORDS

ARPEGGIOS

EXPRESSION

FURTHER
TECHNIQUES

More Arpeggios

Here are arpeggios in some of the new keys we now know.

Look carefully at the fingering, as this will help you move around the keyboard smoothly and without having to jump.

Most arpeggios will fit into one of these fingering patterns.

Have a go at playing through the arpeggios, starting off at a slow pace then gradually building up speed as you master the fingering.

FREE ACCESS on iPhone & Android etc, using any free QR code app

Scan to **HEAR** chords and scales, or go directly to flametreemusic.com

E major arpeggio

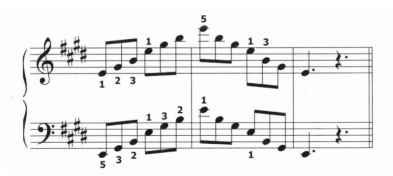

E flat major arpeggio

B flat minor arpeggio

FREE ACCESS on iPhone & Android
etc, using any free QR code app

Scan to **HEAR** chords and scales, or
go directly to flametreemusic.com

FURTHER
TECHNIQUES

Left-hand Techniques

More often than not, you will have a melody in the right hand and need to accompany that melody in the left hand.

Here are a few options; look back at the music you have already played and see if you can spot each technique.

1.   **Single notes.**

2.   **Simple chords.**

3.   **Broken chords and arpeggios.**

4.   **Melodic lines that 'fit in' with the tune.**

Opposite are some examples of left-hand accompaniment styles.

START
HERE

ALL THE
BASICS

RHYTHM
& NOTES

SCALES &
ACCIDENTALS

INTERVALS
& CHORDS

ARPEGGIOS

EXPRESSION

FURTHER
TECHNIQUES

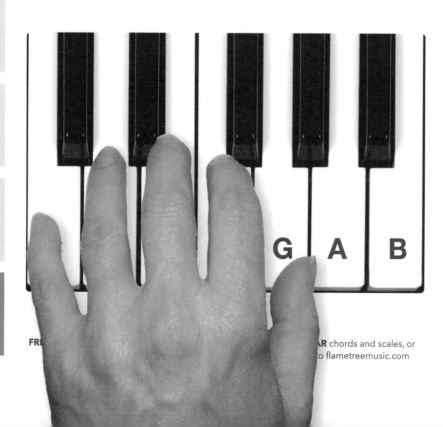

G   A   B

FR... ...R chords and scales, or
...o flametreemusic.com

Simple chordal accompaniment

Bass note plus chord

Broken chord (keeps in hand position)

Arpeggio (uses a wider range on the keyboard)

Broken chord (wider range and with rhythmic pattern)

Bass note and chord (with rhythmic pattern)

START HERE

ALL THE BASICS

RHYTHM & NOTES

SCALES & ACCIDENTALS

INTERVALS & CHORDS

ARPEGGIOS

EXPRESSION

FURTHER TECHNIQUES

FREE ACCESS on iPhone & Android etc, using any free QR code app

Scan to **HEAR** chords and scales, or go directly to flametreemusic.com

What We Know So Far

This section has significantly increased your musical knowledge.

We have covered key signatures up to five sharps and flats, looked at left-hand technique and learned about different styles of music.

That is a lot of information to take in. Read through the following points to remind you about all this.

1. Key signatures have either **sharps** or **flats**.

2. Each key signature represents one **major** and one **minor** key.

3. The **relative minor** is 3 **half-steps** (semitones) **below** the **major**.

4. **Harmonic minor scales** have a **sharpened 7th**.

5. **Chromatic** scales use **all** the black and white **notes**.

6. **Fingering** is important when playing **arpeggios**.

7. There are a small number of common **left-hand techniques** which can be used when **accompanying a melody**.

FURTHER TECHNIQUES

FREE ACCESS on iPhone & Android etc, using any free QR code app

Scan to **HEAR** chords and scales, or go directly to flametreemusic.com

And Finally...

If you go to the Flame Tree Red Book in the Pieces section (online at flametreemusic.com), you will be able to consolidate what you have learned in this section, with extra pieces to play.

There are tunes in the new keys, and some will be in the minor – **look out for accidentals** which may indicate the **sharpened 7th**.

Also look at the **left-hand parts**: see if you can spot the accompaniment techniques you have learned. **Look for chords** and also for **chord shapes** made up from consecutive notes. Are these broken chords?

When you **see** a **row** of **notes**, try to **work out** *which* **scale** they are from. They could be major, minor or chromatic. They will most often come from the scale associated with the key signature of the music.

As always, **practise each hand separately** before then trying to put them together.

Look out for the following signs and and symbols too!

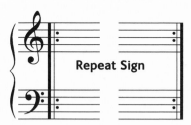

Repeat Sign

The music between these two signs should be repeated. If the first symbol above is not present then you should repeat from the beginning.

Accent

This sign means you should play the note a little louder.

START HERE

ALL THE BASICS

RHYTHM & NOTES

SCALES & ACCIDENTALS

INTERVALS & CHORDS

ARPEGGIOS

EXPRESSION

FURTHER TECHNIQUES

flametreemusic.com

The Flame Tree Music website complements our range of print books and offers easy access to chords and scales online, and on the move, through tablets, smartphones, and desktop computers.

1. The site offers access to chord diagrams and finger positions for both the guitar and the piano/keyboard, presenting a wide range of sound options to help develop good listening technique, and to assist you in identifying the chord and each note within it.

2. The site offers 12 **free** chords, those most commonly used in bands and songwriting.

3. A subscription is available if you'd like the full range of chords, **50** for **each key**.

4. Guitar chords are shown with **first** and **second positions on the fretboard**.

5. For the keyboard, you can **see** and **hear** each note in **left**- and **right-hand positions**.

6. Choose the key, then the chord name from the drop down menu. Note that the **red chords** are available **free**. Those in blue can be accessed with a subscription.

7. Once you've selected the chord, press **GO** and the details of the chord will be shown, with chord spellings, keyboard and guitar fingerings.

8. Sounds are provided in four easy-to-understand configurations.

9. flametreemusic.com also gives you access to **20 scales for each key**.

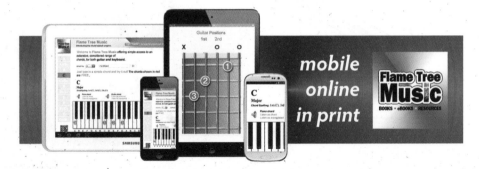